From the

Roaring Deep

A Devotional in Honor of Poseidon
and
the Spirits of the Sea

Edited by Rebecca Buchanan

BIBLIOTHECA ALEXANDRINA

"Poseidon" by Nina Kossman

Dedication: Sailor's Prayer

by Ann Howells

O Spirit of the Sea, who turns the tides with
prestidigitation,
> *Hear us.*

O Spirit of the Sea, who whips the frenzied
waters with a breath,
> *Hear us.*

O Spirit of the Sea, who spits in the eye of the
man in the moon,
> *Hear us.*

O Spirit of the Sea, who gargles through riprap
and blowholes,
> *Hear us.*

O Spirit of the Sea, who juggles ships like red
rubber balls,
> *Hear us.*

O Spirit of the Sea, who enflames night skies
with his great brush,
> *Hear us.*

O Spirit of the Sea, whose chamber lies within
the nautilus,
> *Hear us.*

O Spirit of the Sea, who governs and protects our
watery planet,
> *Hear us.*

That crack of thunder, knell of foghorn shall be
contained,
> *Grant us.*

That all who set to sea in chill pre-dawn return at
nightfall,

> *Grant us.*

That all who live along your shores be blessed,

> *Grant us.*

Introduction

I have never lived near the sea. Rivers and mountains and high plains, yes; but the few years I lived in California were far inland, and I visited the shore only once. I spent an hour walking up and down the beach, huddled inside a thin coat, wishing that I could be someplace warm with a book.

This lack of a connection to the sea on my part translated into a lack of connection with Poseidon. He didn't really interest me. He was the bearded guy who threw up storms and shook the earth when he was pissed and tormented Odysseus and fathered Theseus and, well, that was about it.

Now Iris, on the other hand … ah, yes, I adored Iris. The beauty and ephemeral nature of the rainbow called to me, and I loved the fact that Hera had her own heavenly messenger. When I discovered that, in some genealogies, Iris is the daughter of the marine God Thaumus, my interest in Poseidon accordingly shifted. Maybe there was more to him — and his extensive entourage — than I had initially realized.

And, of course, there was and is so much more to Poseidon and Amphitrite and Triton and Medusa and Tethys and Nereus and the Nereids and Proteus and Styx and Doris and Thaumas and on and on and on the list goes.

They are of the sea, and more than the sea. They are the primordial ocean from which life arose, and which continues to sustain the world. They are the saltwater in our blood. They are storm and wind and tide and crashing waves. They are glorious beings of water and salt and light, avengers of injustice and providers of bounty. They are fathers and mothers and lovers. They are wrathful and exuberant, compassionate and wise, quixotic and impulsive and shrewd.

They are Powers most worthy of our devotion, our prayers, and our respect.

Rebecca Buchanan
Spring 2015

Table of Contents

Appendix C

Spirits of the Deep

"Untitled" by Wayne McMillan

Aphrodite Soteira

by Melia Brokaw

Told by a friend to a friend about a friend ...
A long time ago, in a time far away
A merchant made a fortunate find
in the last port before homeward bound.
Archaic in style and only a span high
a statuette of Aphrodite,
Patroness of Naukratis, his home town.

Carefully wrapped in rugs
tied securely to the main mast
the holds being too full
with bounty from other ports.
The ship set sail
the crew joyously heading home.

Near Egypt, the sky started to storm
the seas started to pitch and boil.
Was it Zeus and Poseidon trading blows?
Or did the sailors forget their offerings?
It matters not, all that matters is the now.
The ship was rocked and tossed,
It was sent up and it was sent down.
It was waved from side to side.
The motion of the ship was so violent
that even the hardiest sailor became sick.

Huddled near the main mast,
Both merchant and crew found themselves
Sick, miserable and afraid.
Visible was the statue
The rugs inexplicably gone.
Oh Aphrodite Euploia, Oh Aphrodite Pontia
Save us from the water depths.
We are your children from Naukratis
Oh Aphrodite Eiplimenia
Deliver us safely home!

Before their very eyes,
the ropes became green myrtle
scenting the air so sweetly
that their stomachs became calm
as did the raging sea and sky.
As the sun warmed their skin
their spirits did rise
for to home, to loved ones
they would return!

As soon as the ship came to rest
in their beloved home port
reverently the Merchant rushed
the savior image and myrtle boughs
to her temple near the docks.
There he gave offerings of thanks
for a safe home coming,
dedicating the statuette to the temple.

A feast of thanksgiving he then threw
for friends, family, and crew
in the temple of Aphrodite
Giving out garlands of the sweet myrtle
That adorned the ship
Calling them Naukratite
And praising Aphrodite's name.

flotsam

by Cailin

we crash like seafoam,
our driftwood bones knee-knocking
across the sheets.

i dive for pearls in your hair,
lose my breath but
your sighs fill my landsick lungs,

our bodies carving castles in the sand.
("you've practiced," you whisper.
"tongues in tidepools have taught you how to
love.")

the moon swells the waves.
your kneecaps are
dolphin noses,
your fingertips, hermit crabs
that scuttle on my skin.

we howl like seaside wolves, and then,
when daybreak comes you're sprawled like yawning
waves
in the early morning tide.

you are a shipwreck.

between sailor's-knotted sheets
we sweat the ocean,
you, a siren,
i, odysseus chained.

graeae

by Ruby Sara

iron and salt – stygian crag and
scale, nosing stink // sand

rotting net
infested // constellations

prophecies littered around its hips
(such hips as a sea serpent
might have)

moon and fish // the black rook shakes
rain out of the shoots,
dead lampreys,

shale, dwindle and muck

do not pass the eye to me
sisters

i have seen
enough

High Tide

by Bill Vernon

Sonoma County, twenty miles north of Jenner and the Russian River, dawn, on the coastal hiking trail, biking in a thick, chilly mist when the bluff gives way beneath my tires. Instincts push me off the machine and roll me toward the inland side away from the roaring surf I can't see but know is high. My stomach and chest strike the earth several times, and bouncing I flail in panic for purchase. The 200-foot tumble knocks me out.

Dream or reality: rocking in the waves, being dragged through the sand, lifted, carried, laid down, warm, enveloping lips, gentle fingers releasing my nose and mouth, sudden cold filling my insides. I wake up coughing in absolute blackness.

"Relax. Take it easy," a voice says.

"Where am I?"

"You're safe. Don't worry."

I try but can't move my arms or legs, can't roll over onto either side, can't turn my head. Is something holding me down? There's no pain, no sensation of weight pressing me. I can't feel my skin-tight workout clothes.

"I'm paralyzed."

"Nothing's wrong. You're out of danger. Sleep and rest and you'll wake up restored."

"I can't sleep. Put a light on, will you? Start a fire. I can't see a thing and I'm freezing."

"We have our body heat. The only light we have is our mind. They're all you need if you use them."

I say, "This is a dream."

"No."

The voice is low and soothing, but indistinguishable as male or female. Its tone and choice of words seem simply generic. What does it mean by "we"? I've heard only one voice. The only breathing I hear is my own. Such a deep blackness covers me that keeping my eyes open is the same as closed. There is a damp, earthy smell, a thick taste of salt in my mouth.

"Why are you here?" asks the voice.

"I fell off the bluff."

Oddly, I'm not worried about my bike. Two thousand dollars worth of equipment, and I just now casually remember it. Normally, the possible loss of such an expensive possession, especially its theft, would upset me and cause obsessive fears.

"That's good. You've changed," says the voice.

Maybe it is good. I've always bought the best of whatever I want and my desire to develop my body into its best possible shape is just an extension of that habit. Today, I tried to prove myself by stupidly bicycling on a slippery, uneven trail, on the edge of a very steep bluff, in a mist, and alone. Do I have a death wish?

23

"Maybe a life wish," the voice says.

That's right. I want to do more than vegetate. I want to fulfill my potentials.

Slowly light has filtered down around me so that now I can see a shaggy dark shape rise from my body and stand there, looking down at me. Its voice says, "No other reason you're here?"

Escaping the rat race, I guess. San Francisco's nice, but life in the city .... The work and the hassles. The crowding. The artificiality of everything sometimes just suffocates me. Its consumerism and hurry and plain old greed seem to be destroying all that is natural and good. Who needs it? I mean sometimes I look across the sparkling, rolling bay at the headlands and the hills and just have to get away.

The light brightens further. Although the figure blocks from view the source of the light, I think I see a human body outlined beneath a long, thick coat of hair. It lies down beside me and says, "Weren't you coming to something more than running away from something?"

"Yes, I was." I feel the wetness now. I'm in the ocean, throbbing in the surf, rising and falling with the water. I say, "I was getting back to something I love and had forgotten."

A wave raises the hairy figure above me, flips it slightly so that its face is illuminated. I stare. Its eyes for a moment are familiar. Then its body slams down upon me so hard it takes my breath away.

I gasp. I'm half buried beneath sand and wave. There is no one else here. Just me. The thing and I have merged. I am for the first time aware of a remnant of a primordial personality that has until now lain vestigial. It's a natural inheritance in my character. The Adam and Eve factor from the beginning.

I feel at home. My stiffened body relaxes. The sun bears down, heating me, and I crawl from the sea to dry land.

Finding Medusa

by Steven Klepetar

They say they found her bones in a burial mound
on Syros, in the Cyclades, a small skull with a trail
of serpent bones mostly crushed to dust, which look
to have been attached. The particular evolutionary
advantage of this specific adaptation has not yet
been determined, but now we know that she lived
in the Mediterranean, just north of The Sea of Crete.
They named her Medusa, of course, and so far none
of the archeologists that looked at her have turned
to stone, though it's likely they will one day, when
their mirrors break and all they have left are
memories of a grisly smile. She was a monster
after all, though really, it's hard to say why
(aside from the turning to stone effect, which
was hardly her fault). Talk about blaming the
        victim –
another rape by the gods, and she gets the hairdo
from hell, snakes resistant to comb and brush,
or even conditioner squeezed from the bodies of
        crabs.
And it's not like she walked around looking for
        people
to transform. If you had to end up on that volcanic
        pile,
with its black dagger rocks to tear at naked feet,
you might have had the sense to stay away from
the cave she shared with those immortal "sisters"

(no blood of her poor mortal self) and even they
no more guilty of death than vipers or eagles or
      sharks.
Turning to stone seems a natural thing, protection
like wolfsbane or monkshead or other poisonous
      plants,
or armor, like a turtle's shell or defensive weapons
like tines on a porcupine's back.
Was she even human then, when the hero's blade
cut that writhing head of horrors at the neck,
and a goddess fashioned a flute to imitate the high
pitched screams she offered, her last sacrifice to
      mist
and sea breeze as her life drained out onto the
      scarring sand?

The Medusa of Midway Diner

by Hillary Lyon

The neon sign came to life twitching and buzzing, birthing the image of the giant jellyfish. Its pink and white tentacles rose and fell in a stiffly staccato motion. The head of the jellyfish wore an improbable smile, and an even more improbable baseball cap. The sign had been an attraction for tourist photographers for more than twenty years. Other than being located within driving distance to the beach, the Midway Diner had nothing to do with jellyfish, or any fish, for that matter; except, perhaps, serving fried fish for Friday's blue-plate special. So the diner's mascot, the giant neon jellyfish the locals called Olly (after the owner and fry-cook), became an attraction in itself, and travelers often ended up eating at the Midway. Needing no other form of advertising, the diner did alright. Of course, having statue garden roadside-attraction on the other side of the parking lot didn't hurt, either.

Families on vacation, truckers, solitary traveling businessmen, hipsters on road-trips, as well as hungry locals, all landed in the Midway at one time or another. As far as diner food went, the menu listed the standard, predictable fare, but what came out of the kitchen was wonderful. And the service was stellar, especially if you were lucky enough to have 'lissa as your waitress.

That's no typo; she spelled her name apostrophe little l-i-s-s-a. Maybe it was short for Melissa, maybe it was a fanciful spelling of Lisa, maybe it was entirely made up when she was a teen searching for an identity. It was unique to her, and that's what she wanted. She never became annoyed when folks asked her about the spelling; in fact, she liked the attention it brought her. The world, she said, is full of too many people sharing the same names. Where's the individuality? We might as well all be named John and Jane.

* * *

"It's not an octopus or squid," 'lissa was saying as she delivered her table's plates, "though most tourists think it's one or the other. It's actually a jellyfish."

The family at the table smiled and nodded and dug into their meals. They didn't care, one way or the other, what the neon creature was; they only wanted a photo and a filling lunch.

"Olly — that's what we locals call him — was created by the renowned Mexico City neon artist, Reynaldo. The *Reynaldo*. You've probably read about him online, or maybe saw that documentary on him that aired on PBS a few years back. *A Life in Lurid Light*. No? Hmm. You should look him up, he's an awesome talent."

The family nodded and smiled, and continued to chew.

"Reynaldo was passing thorough on vacation," 'lissa explained, "and stopped in for lunch. I, myself, was his waitress. And let me tell you, he's one good-lookin' fella! He was so taken by our food and, uh, 'ambiance' as he put it, that he insisted on creating a sign for us. He donated it! Imagine having a world class piece of art for your sign, and you didn't have to pay a penny for it! We were so thankful, so the boss said he could eat here for free, for the rest of his natural life! Least he could do."

The family smiled and nodded, and one child said, through a mouthful of french fries: "I'd love that! Maybe I'll be an artist when I grow up! Free food!"

His older sister elbowed him as she giggled through her bite of cheeseburger. The parents just shook their heads at their silly kids. No one stopped eating.

"Well, remember, my name's 'lissa," their waitress said, pointing to her red and white plastic name tag. "If you need anything else, raise your hand and give a wave. I'll be over in a flash." Then 'lissa turned on her heel and bounced back to the counter.

* * *

The last customer of the night rolled in a little before 10:00. He sat down at the counter, stretching his long arms and grunting to catch 'lissa attention. It worked; she looked up from her crossword puzzle and scurried over to him.

"Welcome to the Midway Diner! Can I get you a drink while you look over our menu?"

"Yeah, sure, an ice tea would be nice, darlin'," the customer replied, flashing 'lissa a smile full of chalk-white teeth.

"Okey dokey, sugar, I'll be right back with that," she said before turning away.

The volley of flirtation between the two continued through the stranger's meal. He seemed to want conversation, and 'lissa, as always, wanted the attention.

Finished with his chicken fried steak and collard greens, the stranger pushed his clean plate away and motioned for 'lissa to come over once more. She practically skipped to him.

"So, cutie, what's the deal with the giant neon jellyfish outside?" the stranger asked. "I could see the thing blinking in the distance for miles before I got here. It's like it called to me."

This was the perfect opening for 'lissa to perform her well-practiced spiel. The stranger listened, and nodded, and asked all the right questions to keep her talking.

'So you all call it Olly, though really it should be called Medusa,' the stranger pointed out.

'Medusa?' 'lissa replied, perplexed. 'Like that gal from mythology who had a scalp full of snakes instead of hair? Who'd turn men to stone if they looked at her wrong? Not very family-friendly, is it? Olly is a much nicer name for a restaurant mascot. Besides, it's wearing a hat and a smile!'

'True,' he countered, 'but jellyfish are called Medusa because their tendrils resemble long strands of hair, hair that waves gracefully in the water, slowly dancing with the ebbs and flows of the current."

"Well aren't you the poet!" 'lissa laughed, her eyes twinkling. "Making such a dangerous creature out to be a little thing of beauty. Sure, it's a pretty sight alright, but you don't want to touch them. Ever. They'll sting the living daylights out of you!"

"Granted," her customer continued, "but what woman wouldn't love to have that super power?"

"What power? Stinging hair?" 'lissa giggled.

"No, no, no, no," the stranger laughed. "Turning men who harass you into stone."

"Well, that seems kinda harsh, if you ask me." 'lissa replied uncomfortably. "I mean, if somebody's hassling me real bad, I just tell my boss. Or threaten to call the cops."

"But what if there's no time, or you're all by yourself?"

Now 'lissa got spooked by the turn the conversation took. Without a word, she pulled out her pad and tore off his bill, sliding it across the counter to the stranger.

"You know," the stranger said as she began to walk away, "a goddess gave her snakes for hair not to make her a monster, but to protect her."

'lissa stopped, and turned around.

"How so?" she asked, interested. She kept her distance.

"Well, the story goes, Medusa was so beautiful she attracted the unwanted attention, if you catch my drift, of Poseidon. In today's legal terms, we'd say he sexually assaulted her. So the goddess Athena, who felt sorry for her, gave her snake hair, and the ability to change men into stone. To protect her from further harm." The stranger drank the last of his tea, and rattled the remaining ice cubes.

"She was in no way a monster," he continued. "She was actually very sad and lonely. But as often happens with people who are outcasts, they become shadowy figures to be feared. She hid away from human society. And then some macho men decided to make their reputations by taking her down. Many failed, but one did, eventually. Or so I've read."

'lissa didn't know what say. What an odd story he shared with her. She relaxed, but was now suspicious of her customer. What was he getting at?

"You know," he said softly, "you're much too pretty to be working in a small-time diner."

'lissa blushed and pushed a stray tendril of brown hair back under the green silk scarf she wore at work. It came loose again and fell back into her face when she leaned over to gather the dirty dishes.

He reached over to touch her left hand. "And

no wedding ring? Hard to believe no one's snatched you up."

She changed the subject. "So how do you know so much about Medusa? You a professor, or something?"

He tilted his head cute like a puppy. "No, I'm in nautical sales. Just interested in old stories, that's all."

"Bet you're a real mover and shaker."

"Oh, yeah," he laughed, "I make tsunamis and all manner of ocean storms. Gotta punish those who would defile the seas."

"Uh huh," 'lissa answered distractedly as she wiped the counter top.

"Why don't you meet me outside when you get off work," the stranger proposed. "We can drive down to the beach, go for a moon light stroll — "

" — get swallowed by a giant wave, dragged out to sea, and disappear," she interrupted.

"My, you are a feisty one," he laughed.

"And you're not fooling anybody, Mr. Traveling-Salesman-But-Not-Really. I'm getting awfully tired of this game. How did you find me?"

He sighed, and his breath smelled of decaying fish in polluted water. "Your great neon sign, Mister Olly. A beacon in the night. Flashing with a heart-beat rhythm, telling me across the miles, 'here she is, here she is, here she is.'"

"*She's* been here more than ten years. You just now find me, or just now started looking?" 'lissa undid the scarf around her head, and shook

34

loose her wavy hair. Under the fluorescent light of the diner, it seemed to undulate ever so slightly. In that moment, she went from pretty to stunning.

The stranger cracked his knuckles and laughed. "We don't have to fight. You could come along quietly — "

" — and get knocked up? Have you bail when I'm about to pop? No thanks." As 'lissa became more agitated, her hair clumped into dreadlocks and began to squirm. Tiny sparks flashed on the ends coalescing into tiny eyes. Needle fangs sprouted in tiny mouths.

"I think you need to go while you can still move," 'lissa quietly threatened.

"You can't harden a god."

"You're not a god," 'lissa whispered though a tight smile. "You're a wannabe hero. Poseidon is a god, and he lost interest in me a long time ago, thank you Athena. There's a reason why she's the goddess of wisdom. Shame on you, impersonating your betters. Shame on you, thinking I'm stupid just because you've read Ovid and *assume* that I haven't. Shame on you for attempting to lure me to my doom, like I'm some easy slattern." Her eyes sparked like a roman candle, set alight by self-righteous fury.

And that was that. The stranger froze in mid-stoop as he rose from the counter stool, his hand reaching inside his jacket. Was he reaching for his wallet, a cell phone, a weapon, or — most likely, a mirror? 'lissa didn't know or care.

35

She leaned close to the statue's surprised face. "Ovid got the story right, for the most part. Except for that bit about Perseus, that 'hero' who took me down. I gave that poet permission to use his license. A mirror employed in ending me? Clever, though an easy out. Ovid and I both benefited, didn't we? He's still read two thousand years later, and I'm still walking the Earth. Which is more than I can say for you, at this point." She shoved her wiggling hair back up under her scarf, and called out to Olly.

"Hey, boss, we got another one for your statue garden."

The Mermaids

by Rachel V. Olivier

Salt seasons the summer breeze,
spices up the odors of seaside
roses and forsythias.
Gulls arc out over the water with ease,
proclaiming their lonely cry —
a prayer for the ages.
Waves hit the rocky shore
slapping and sucking at the piers.
Buoys toll out across the water,
marking the frame for a door.
A portal is forming as the time nears;
the world waits for the daughters.
Every year about this time
they walk along the railroad tracks
that run by the edge of Bellingham Bay.
Their flashing hair a kind of sign
like so many nautical flags
on the arrival of Opening Day.
Eyes echoing the lights and colors
of the sea before them, they sing.
These are the daughters of Nereus and Doris,
drinking the holy communion of their order.
Perched on the rocks by the water ringed.
Their voices joined in chorus.
They sing their sad songs.
They sing their love songs.
They sing their sailors home from the sea.

The sailboats skim along.
Fishing boats chug through the sound.
A vision of toys all shiny.
The mermaids sit on the rocks and sing.
Balanced in the crux of creation and destruction.
These daughters of Nereus and Doris and Sea
along the railroad tracks are walking.
Hearts and souls in contemplation
Of the lives for which they plead.

Kybele's Naiads

by Melia Brokaw

A powerful ally had they,
the Trojan ships of Aeneas.
The Mother of the Gods, no less.
For when the Rutulians flung
greedy torches at hulls of pine,
She recalled their holy source
Her very own grove on Mt. Ida.

So with the shrill of flutes
and the loud clash of cymbals
Kybele flew to their rescue
in her lion drawn chariot
screaming, "sacrilege shall not
devour my holy limbs."

The goddess's words
became drumming thunder
followed by dancing hailstones
intermixing with stomping rain.
Winds, warring like brothers,
brought tumult and confusion.

"You! Bring me those ropes!"
She commanded the angry winds.
Using these lines the Lady forced
the burning ships to plunge

deep into Poseidon's realm
where no ships should go.

Blue painted wood became flesh,
prows curved into heads,
oars shifted into long lithe legs,
while keels grew into spines,
lines split into flowing locks and
sail yards developed into arms.

Where frightened ships were
now only blue naiads are seen
cavorting gaily in the sea.
Born on a mountain side,
but forever more found
in the watery deep.

This is why young sailor,
Naiads help ships at sea,
as they remember the dangers.
But They are also angry still.
Sail not upon Greek ships
Or an early grave you will have.

Neptune's Daughter

by Matthew Wilson

"Lady, you're crazy. I'm not going out there," Mitch said when the woman came running down the beach, screaming.

"My daughter!" Jessica wailed, clawing at him. "She was sleeping on a surfboard and the water came in — God, I only closed my eyes — she's only six! You have to help me."

Mitch liked the beach atmosphere. Giving jet-ski rides to kids for ten dollars an hour was a breeze, a quick money-making scheme. His dad had threatened to throw him out unless he earned money with a summer job. He'd been an idiot to spend his inheritance from his aunt on a jet-ski ... maybe now he could make some lodging money with it. Today had been productive. In just five hours, Mitch had made over $250. His old man hadn't made a tenth of that in a whole week of his first job. Mitch couldn't wait to see that old trout's face. Mitch had been so happy. And now this.

He squinted over the golden ocean. The sun was low.

"It — it's too late," Mitch said, but Jessica was already jumping onto the black leather seat behind him. There was no time for a helmet or the usual safety talk.

"Go, go!" she demanded. "I'll give you all my savings. Everything — just help her!"

Maybe Jessica would give him enough of a reward to buy a new house away from his dad's oppressive thumb. Rich-wigs came to this place every day to bronze. Jessica said her daughter was only six. A shame. On the news, Mitch saw kids die every day in wars and famine. It wasn't his concern; he was trying to make his own peaceful way in the world and didn't want to get involved.

Not when Lady Rain would be awake.

Jessica kicked her feet against the motor like a cowgirl bringing her heels sharply into the side of her horse. "Come on, what's the hold up?"

Mitch still stared at the water. Yes, all child deaths were a gruesome subject. But maybe the sea would not get one of them.

"Damn it," he cursed and started the engine. "Hold on, then."

Jessica gave him directions, figuring the tide would take Eve out on a straight line from her starting point. Hopefully, she slept still on that damn board. Better that than be awake and alone, terrified. What if she tried to swim back or fell overboard in her anxiety? Jessica wailed again at the thought her of baby out there in the near dark.

Mitch only feared one thing. Of course, his father had told him never to trust the sea. Fisherman had been disappearing for centuries, but it was a local legend they never told visitors. This place relied on outsiders to boost it's funding for hospitals and schools, and that would dry up if no one came to admire the beach.

True, two tourists vanished back in 2003, but that was put down to cramps after the men on a stag-do were seen eating heavily moments before entering the water. No one spoke of Neptune's daughter. Lady Rain.

"There! There!" Jessica suddenly became animated and threatened to tip them both in the water when she saw a black dot illuminated against the last of the light.

"Alright," Mitch said, turning the handle bars before her slaps bruised his kidney. The problem with a productive day was that he was very low on fuel. If the lady had given him half a minute to breathe, he'd have refueled before departing. But she had been quite persistent.

Mitch slowed the jet-ski so the water the engines threw up didn't knock the little girl off the board. She was still sleeping, curled up two miles off shore like a napping puppy beside the fire.

"Honey!" Jessica squealed and threw herself off the machine before Mitch had completely stopped.

"Hey!"

Damn it. She was making too much noise. He was happy the little girl was okay, but this was taking too long. It was too dark. Lady Rain would be awake. A blob of seaweed on the surface set his teeth so tight that he cracked two molars before a flash of agonising pain made him realise what he was doing.

Dad had warned him that the old mermaid used a net on her victims just like her father, dragging them down to her bed of bones. Mariners back in whaling times had thrown harpoons at her, leaving her body covered in angry red scars. Her injuries had ruined her beauty and made her hate all men on these waters. She'd made it her long life's goal to find and drown them.

Mitch watched the water and felt close to pissing himself.

The sea swallowed the sun entirely and only cold starlight remained to illuminate the way back.

"C'mon, lady! Damn!"

Eve woke with a snap when Jessica doggy paddled forward and took her arm.

"Mommy, where are we?"

Mitch restarted the engine. He wouldn't like himself in the morning, but he would leave them behind if he had to. "Come on, come on."

"Whats the rush?" Jessica demanded.

Mitch knew she wouldn't believe him. He didn't care if she thought him arrogant. So long as he was alive. "Go now, move. Go." He kicked water at her and she dragged the surfboard in one hand. She'd be fined fifty dollars by the renting folks for not fetching it back. "Forget the board, just get the kid."

Jessica released the surfboard. "What, is there a weight issue with these jet-ski things?"

"Mommy, I'm scared."

"It's alright, honey," Jessica cooed, lifting Eve into the seat with her. "This man is our friend. He's here to help —"

Jessica had to hold on for dear life when Mitch hit the gas and nearly threw them backward into the water like a tumbling gymnast. "Slow down!" Jessica screamed, coughing as the engine threw up water like a spitting dolphin. "You're gonna crash us!"

Mitch knew these waters like the backs of his hands. And the things that waited beneath them. He was crying worse than Eve when they hit the shore. He didn't help Jessica and the child off the back of the beached machine. He threw himself forward over the handle-bars like a dog performing tricks and didn't stop until he was on solid ground. Where Lady Rain could not get him.

Jessica covered her daughter's ears and cursed him. She advanced like hot thunder, grateful he had saved their lives, but immediately halved the reward money she'd promised. Mitch didn't care. He'd done what his father had demanded he not do — and what rebellious child at heart could resist that?

The girl was safe and he'd not been dragged down into that deep dark cold of Lady Rain's bed. He wiped his eyes dry and called himself a fool for being so worried. He'd heard no mocking laughter which the stories said marked the mermaid's presence. He hadn't seen so much as a flick of fin. Maybe dad was messing with him. Punishment for

45

being a burden under his feet. Parents did use stories to scare their children into doing the things they wanted.

Steps bolder, Mitch returned to the water, waving Jessica and Eve good-bye as they headed for their hotel and dry clothes. Today had been exciting, but how would he make a profit if he let the tide take out his jet-ski as easily as it had this child? He had to drag it further along the beach and cover it up in case of rain. Sand got everywhere — it would be no good with clogged gears.

"Come on, girl," Mitch said as he locked his knees and pulled the machine up along the wet sand.

The light was poor so his first reaction as his leg nudged something wet and sticky was to shriek.

More seaweed?

Thick and black as spider's silk, it was tangled around the rear propellers.

It was a net, with two human skulls.

The Nereids

by Callum Hurley

O fairest nymphs of Haliad, fifty of name
O Oceanic cataract high
I sing of thee, commit thy names in verse
By Muses breath, lent to my own
That by my hand, may be forgot not one
In the deeply hearts of men;

Greatest Lady Amphitrite, Magnificent Queen of
circling third, stiller of ramage, consort of Poseidon,
ether-born, sacrament of seas, eternally-shifting,
eternally-whole, bringer of peace to licentious tides,
may your glory be above all

Fairest Thetis, Of Greatest renown, mother of
Achilles, protector of Zeus and carer for Gods,
many formed and Silver-Footed, of Ocean-born,
may you rightly be praised

Ladies Kymatolege and Kymodoke, Sisters of
Amphtrite, noble stillers of violent swells, may you
have kind mercy upon the sailor

Lady Thoe, Of surging water, of carrying ships,
may your kind hand bring voyages home

Lady Polynome, Many-pastured, by your mien
fruits the fields of Sea

Lady Pronoe, Of forethought, known to thee the currents path

Lady Proto, Of the first-voyage, may you carry men to homes and pastures new

Lady Speio, Of caves, her havens and wombs of water all

Lady Menippe, Of strongest horses, you are crashing waves and waters white

Lady Halia, Of the brine, found in the pickled taste of salt

Lady Doto, Safe-voyager, giver of abundance, may you grant passage cross the waves

Lady Amphithoe, Of currents, who so swiftly moves and circles the world

Lady Eumolpe, Of songs at sea, Oceanic Muse, may you bring joy to men

Lady Dexamene, Of Strength of hand, be given to the sweat of sailors

Lady Apseudes, Of the ocean air, pure and healing, may you be our breath

Lady Neso, Of Islands, crops of land both great and humble

Lady Psamathe, Of Golden Sands, given thee warm beaches and soothing rest

Lady Themisto, Of the Ocean's law, great bringer of order to chaos fluid

Lady Dynamene, Of the Ocean's fury, your sound is the untamed crash of Hippocampi's hooves

Lady Thalia, Of the blooming seas, colours and creatures vast and goodly

Lady Polynoe, Of the rich mind, yours wise and wide as the sea

Lady Nausithoe, Of swift ships, held firm in your hands of wind

Lady Maera, Of gentle waves, may you give soft caresses of the mightiest hand

Lady Klymene, Of fame, your renown that spans the vastly blue

Lady Kallianeira, Of the ocean sun, scattered jewels that shimmer bright

Lady Melite, Of stilled waves, of the peace that dwells in change

Lady Galenea, Of the calmest seas, may you be the ship's cradle

Lady Nesiae, Guardian of islands, may you protect us against the untamed wrath

Lady Pasithea, All-divine, of the Godly deeps

Lady Ploto, Of Sailing ships, the fairest wind the shakes the canvas

Lady Eudora, Of fine gifts, pearls and corals bright

Lady Sao, Of the rescue of those lost at sea, o merciful saver of life

Lady Amatheia, Nursemaid of fish, lilting, vein of the abyss

Lady Laegore, Of the schooling fish, the bringing of her children

Lady Hippothoe, Of noble stallions, waves swift and fierce

Lady Kymothoe, Of the running waves, your horses roam the seas

Lady Nemertes, Of unerring counsel, wisest and justest amongst Sisters

Lady Erato, The lovely, show to we the essence of the Oceans grace

Lady Pherusa, Of the carrying wave, bearing men and drifting creatures all

Lady Panopeia, Of Panorama, lain vast and broad to horizons verge

Lady Lyssianassa, Of Royal delivery, may thine regality twixt port and call

Lady Protomedia, The first Queen, she of the seas primordia

Lady Agaue, The illustrious, regal and stately matron bright

Lady Eukrante, Of successful voyages, ships returned to home with health and spice

Lady Amphinome, Of surrounding pastures, kind lover of the bountied deep

Lady Aktaie, Of the seashore, boundary ebb and flux, and the life-giving tide

Lady Galuke, Of Blue-Grey waters, you are the astrolabe to depths not known

Lady Plexaure, Of the twisting winds, which whip the surface into mist

Lady Galatea, Of the milky white, union of the sea and sky

Be praised, great maidens, and grant you favour to the seafarer
Now that I have remembered you, and in another song too.

Nereids and Naughty Ponies

by Suzanne Thackston

Ponies running, wild and cunning, racing, racing to
    the shore.
Girls are riding, deftly guiding, fighting to be at the
    fore.

Girls are giggling, shrieking, wriggling, urging on
    their milk-white steeds.
Teasing, taunting, brazen flaunting, daring death-
    defying deeds.

Ponies fighting, kicking, biting, wicked eyes are
    gleaming green,
Now they're dashing, rearing, crashing, smash
    themselves to smithereens.

In the water, Ocean's daughters, flounder breathless
    in the foam.
Amphitrite, lovely, mighty, smiles and calls her
    children home.

Ponies shattered, sleek forms scattered, sucked back
    out into the sea.
Nereids follow, lazy wallow, floating in the waves'
    debris.

Bodies swirling, forming, firming, gleaming flanks
    and tossing manes,

Waves are growing, green and flowing, laughing
　　girls will ride again.

Now it's shoreward, gallop forward, nereids and
　　ponies, too.
Endless turning, green waves churning, dying to be
　　born anew.

Hymn to Nereus I

by Rebecca Buchanan

Greybeard of the Sea
      who comes in the surge
      and retreat of dark waves
Cunning Wonderworker
Father of fifty daughters
      who share his gifts
      of prophecy and truthful speech
Nereus
Salt-Tongued
Wiseman of the Deep

The Nether Waters

by James B. Nicola

As still as nether waters seem;
as cool and soft, moonfire;
as innocent, a walking dream
and calm, the evening air;

as easy as it is to tame
the animal beguiled:
this transient indigo's the same
as when the waters boiled.

While stars send lucifers of lights
a soft breeze starts to rise;
the Altogether reignites
a memory of sighs.

I think that I smell jasmine — or
am I imagining? — ;
I feel that I've set sail once more
to life, to everything,

to you, who made the coolness warm
then made the waters rage
until the echo of a storm
restored me to an age.

The Stygian depths are stilled, of course,
and sailing's safe till dawn.

But I'm amazed how clear nights force
me yet to wonder on

what wake of stirs and currents there
might be, less innocent
than they appear, to take me where
the wilder waters went.

What Proteus Said:
An Incantation

by Jeffrey Beck

Scam me with rotted seal skin —
jam me in a wave of membranes —
a wreck of a coat in a fleck of coasts
in a fractal of unending refrains.

Home's a moon, a mortar, pestle,
a cavern adjoined to a castle,
a fleet uncounted by ten tongues,
swirling dregs in a blind man's vessel.

Snuffing hogs,
spotted cats,
growing trees,
ruffing dogs,
grotted bats,
flowing seas,
this, your human
menagerie.

Your ship's wheel spins an unknowable span
of circles in circles of a woman and man.

She weaves and unweaves weft
thread, grieving moons on her reft
bed, waiting a man who stays or leaves
or comes alive, dying, or half-dead.

Your beard, your answer (please)
will unknit her brow and slack her knees.
The tonic fit of hips in a chemise
will launch you home on ship or trapeze.

Roaring lions,
rooting goats,
growing trees,
warring scions,
shooing shoats
flowing seas,
this, your human
menagerie.

Your ship's wheel spins an unknowable span
of circles in circles of a woman and man.

Your main-sail's a strand in a skein
of a hawser, and your ship's lost
in a drip of a spring of a dowser,
and no harbor, none!, can ever house her.

Your ship's wheel spins an unknowable span
of circles in circles of a woman and man.

Styx

by Mab Jones

I swore upon your river, once. Obsidian ribbon
at my feet. Your waters silent witness to my vow.

Older than the gods, you heard. Took my words
and held them tight. Dirt that might produce a pearl,

if I kept my pledge. I trembled as I spoke to you,
my face reflected in your rill as if it was a mirror,

made of oil or ink. My own eyes formed of onyx.
I imagined they were yours. Stone-hard, set in
white,

the parchment of my face; the mouth my autograph,
lips as thin as a snake's. Later on, you learned I'd
lied,

though I think you always knew. Your slim arms
winding around me. My breath, withering fast.

A Wrap for Tethys

by Jennifer Lawrence

Tethys, to Athena at Her loom:

"I ask you for a shawl the color
Of a mermaid's grave:
Blend together all the shades
Of deepest ocean wave.
No pearl or coral to spangle it,
No whitecap and no foam —
Just the colors of the cavern that is
Proteus' bleak home.
The deepest emerald beds of kelp,
The dark before the dawn —
The indigo of night-hued trench
Where demon-fishes spawn;
The blackest blue of storm clouds,
Alight with Tesla's eerie fire —
The swirling typhoon clouds that wreak
Father Poseidon's ire —
No lighter shallows, teal or blue,
No turquoise waves for me,
Just the darkest trenches to be found
Alive beneath the sea."

"The Heralds of Neptune: A Natural History of Tritons" (from Gaspar Schott's 'Oddities of Nature')

translated by Darius Klein

The Ocean produces just as many monsters as the land, as we shall demonstrate in this chapter. We shall discuss those who are humanoid in form and those whose status – human or animal – is ambiguous. Let us begin with the Tritons, which are said to be human in the upper portion of their bodies, all the way down to the navel, but fish in the lower – for which reason they are sometimes called "mermen".

A number of authors have stated that pisciform humans of this kind (whether one calls them Tritons, mermen, or any other suitable designation) have been seen in various times and places. Pliny gives an account of one in Book IX, Chapter 5 of his *Natural History*. In this account, Prince Tiberius that a group of legates had been sent to Olyssiponensis because a Triton was seen in a grotto, playing a conch. In the same chapter, Pliny also states: "I know of authors of the equestrian class, all men of good repute, who saw a merman in the Atlantic Ocean. Its entire body conformed in shape to what is generally understood about such creatures. The men saw him climb aboard a boat during the night, and the part of the boat in which he sat was immediately weighed down. If the creature had not returned to the water, its weight probably would have submerged the vessel."

Pausanias mentions these creatures in Book IX of his *Description of Greece*. However, his description of their physical composition differs in some ways from other accounts. "The temple of

Dionysius," he writes, "is worth a visit, since Calamis constructed it from Parian marble. But the image of the Triton within it is the greater wonder. In the more impressive of the two versions of the Triton legend, the women of Tanagra went down to the sea before the orgies of Dionysius to be purified, where a Triton attacked them while they were swimming. They prayed to Dionysius to come to their aid. The god, so the legend goes, heard their cries and overcame the Triton in a battle. In the lesser of the two versions, the account strains credulity to a lesser extent. A Triton would waylay all the cattle of the people and drive them into the sea. It also attacked small vessels. The people of Tanagra set out a bowl of wine for him, which he drank, attracted by its aroma. He then flung himself on the strand and slept, so that a man from Tanagra was able to chop off his head with an axe. It is for this reason that the image of the Triton in the temple has no head; and because the monster was drunk when the Tanagran killed it, the people suppose that it was Dionysius himself who did the deed. In Rome I saw actual Tritons; they were smaller in size than the images in the temple in Boeotia. Their appearance was as follows. On their heads they grew hair similar to that grown by marsh frogs, not only in its color, but also in the trait of the inseparability of the strands; the rest of their body has rough scales like those of a shark. They had gills under their ears, but a human nose, but the mouth is broader than an ordinary human mouth and its teeth are like those of an animal. Their eyes were blue, and their hands, fingers and nails were of a hard substance like the shell of the murex. Beneath the torso is a tail like a dolphin's instead of two legs and feet."

Aside from what the ancient authors recorded, there are more recent accounts of Tritons. Alexander of Alexandria, in Book III, Chapter 8 of his *Festival Days*, states that Draconetto Boniface, a nobleman of Naples, famous for his knowledge of a wide range of subjects, "was known to relate that, while he was campaigning in Spain, he saw a merman which was entirely human in its face and body above the pubic region, but whose lower half tapered off into a fish's tail. It was brought from the waters of the Atlantic Ocean off the coasts of Morocco, so that the princes under whom he served as general of a battalion could admire it. The creature had the face of an old man, with shaggy hair and a wild beard of a blue color. It was considerably larger than an ordinary human being. It had thin, cartilaginous fins, with which it could swim through the ocean, and a translucent membrane covered its entire frame. Many other noblemen besides Draconetto had a chance to view this creature."

The same author adds the following account: "There is a spring of inexhaustible water in Epirus to which a tale is attached which should be recorded for posterity. The village women came regularly to this spring. A Triton, or merman, observed them from the vantage point of a cave nearby; and if it saw one approaching the spring alone, it leapt out from the watery depths of its grotto and bore the woman away to its lair for the purpose of raping her. When this behavior had become widely-known to the local inhabitants, they captured the creature with a noose. They held it captive for some time, but it was unable to live for long outside of water. It refused all food and at last wasted away from the filth of its living quarters and general inactivity. Tritons are reputed to be lustful, especially for human women; and for this reason the women of the village were prohibited from fetching water from the spring unless accompanied by a man. We accept other accounts from persons who have traveled overseas to diverse places, where they have seen these monsters frolicking in calm waters, and where sailors have encountered them lifting their heads above the waters and speaking in audible voices."

The examples of these accounts prove that Tritons exist, and the facts that they relate find support in the works of other authors: Book IV of Conrad Gesner's *Aquatic Animals*; Dialog 9 of Simon Majoli's *Dog Days*; Book II, Chapter 34 of Francisco Torreblanca's *Disquisitions on Magic*; Book V, Chapter 14 of Juan Eusebio Nieremberg's *Natural History*; the works of Ulisse Aldrovandi; and others. At the end of the first volume of his *Sea Voyages*, Giovanni Battista Ramusio recalls that, during the voyage of Hanno the Carthaginian, the cadaver of a fish very similar in form to a human being was found on the African shore, not far from the Cape of Good Hope. But, although similar in likeness, it was far greater in size than an ordinary man, and its skin was covered with scales composed of rough hairs. In Book XXI, Chapter 1 of his *History of the Northern Peoples*, Olaus Magnus told of a certain marine monster in the Baltic Sea which had a human face and an appendage resembling a monk's caul.

Guillaume Rondelet, quoting Gesner, also documented this creature: "Among the various marine monsters is one that was taken captive during our own time in a stormy sea off the coast of Norway. All who saw it gave it called it 'The Monk'. Its face was human, albeit wild and savage; its head was smooth and hairless; and its shoulders came together as if they formed the caul of a monk. It had two long fins instead of arms, and its lower parts ended in a wide tail, widest in the middle, which resembled a military uniform. The Most Illustrious Margaret, Queen of Navarre, gave this creature to me as a gift. She had received it from a certain nobleman who had brought a similar creature to Charles V during his employment in Spain. He told the queen that he had seen this monster captured in Norway after the waves had cast it ashore following a violent storm; he cited the locale as Die Zundt, next to the town of Den Elepoch. Gisbert the Physician showed me an illustration of this monster, which had been sent to him from Norway while he was at Rome. The illustration differed in some ways from my own. Accordingly, I believe that the illustrator added certain details which were not exactly accurate, so that his audience might find the creature even more wonderful. I thus believed that his monster resembled the human form because it had been manufactured from the parts of frogs, whose characteristic musculature could be detected around either side of the head in that structure intended to represent a monk's caul. Its skin, moreover, was not scaly, but rather thick and wrinkled, exactly like that of a sea lion."

Should he take an interest, the reader can find many other examples of this kind in the works of Pierre Belon and Gesner. Pierre Gilles, in his *Zoology*, also quoted by Peter the Spaniard, relates that a Triton was brought to King Renato. Juan Luis Vives states that in the Netherlands a merman was seen by many people and held captive over the space of two years. The creature was mute, but when it attempted to speak it was allowed to return to the water, to its great happiness. Luigi Guicciardo describes a similar animal in his *Description of Belgium*, in a passage which Majoli cites. During the papacy of Eugene IV, a merman was captured near the city of Shebenik, in Albania. The creature had been attempting to drag a child into the sea. It withdrew beneath the waves when it was wounded by the stones of those who had come to the child's rescue. Its appearance was almost human, except that its skin was like that of an eel, and it had two horns sticking out from its head. Its hands were bisected to form two appendages in lieu of fingers, and its lower half consisted of two membranous tails resembling the wings of a bat.

Majoli, Nieremberg, and many other authors attest that a certain Mena, a provincial governor in Egypt, encountered two creatures of nearly human appearance in the Nile Delta as he was walking past the river at sunrise. One of the creatures was male, the other female. The male was barrel-chested, had a fierce expression and tangled hair, and was naked all the way to the pubic area. The female had breasts, a feminine face, and abundant hair. The entire local populace saw these creatures up until the ninth hour of the morning, an occurrence which Mena described in an epistle to Emperor Maurice. According to Majoli, the Abbot Theophanes the Confessor gave an account of the same event in his *Chronology*.

Majoli, Rondelet, and Belon, citing Aldrovandi and Gesner, claim that a merman was captured in the Baltic Sea in 1531 and presented as a gift to King Sigismund. Its bodily shape was similar in appearance to that of a Bishop wearing his habit.

Peter Martyr d'Anghiera, in his *Geography of the New World*, describes a merman found in the West Indies. "We have already said that Ataia is a region near Chiribchen, noteworthy for its salt mines. Whoever looks out over the sea of this region can see creatures swimming there, sometimes playing and sometimes at rest. The people there have all claimed that these creatures have human heads with hair and dense beards. Whenever they observe the creatures in silence, they swim about in a purposeful way; but when they shout at them, the creatures are terrified by the sound and dive under the waves, showing the lower parts of their bodies in the process. In this way it is possible to see that the lower half of the creatures tapers off into tail like that of a fish. By beating their tails against the otherwise tranquil water, the creatures are able to cause hard waves to beat against the shore. We think that these creatures are Tritons, whom the ancients called the Heralds of Neptune."

"Iris" by Louise Élisabeth Vigée le Brun

Bound Golden Wings:
A Winter Solstice Letter

by Rachel Petersen

O Iris, dear radiant, golden goddess, what has
       happened?
Why does Elder Winter bind Your wings? Does His
       frost bring You sorrow?
Your rain falls cold, Your flames are dimmed
The dark Season chokes the bright Sunrays that
       should warm You
and Your rain, Your flames,
they freeze the Earth and melt into mud and street
       salts
You, too, must be pining for Persephone, stolen
       woman,
as all Nature does in the dark Season

No doubt You are still busy
Though Your glow is muted, Your wings pale,
a messenger's work is never done, is it?
and rain, frozen or not, must still nourish us
Your perseverance inspires me, bold Iris, as do the
brilliant holiday lights
as they sparkle in ice and glass
and burn through the cold and dark which bind us

I shall let the sleeping trees lie quiet now
and stand instead with the evergreens as they lift
Stars and Angels

who carry the Sun's burdens
while the Clouds, Your kin, huddle for warmth
and march, in solemn procession, in search of the
       Maiden,
Demeter's daughter, frosty Queen, carrier of Spring
       desires

I hum songs of light to You, dear Iris
May they lift Your golden wings!

Hymn to Iris III

by Rebecca Buchanan

she descends
in her many-hued skirt
dewed breasts shimmering
beloved of sun and storm
evanescent one

iris

Praised be the Rainbow

by Rachel Petersen

Hear me, Iris, brilliant Speaker,
Rainbow Woman, storming feet, swift wings!
Thy presence is ever welcomed, o golden Iris!
Thy beauty stills my breath, stirs my heart
Thy skills are without rival, o celestial Artist
Organic gold are Thy wings, Thy robes
The air is sweetened by Thy laughter,
Thy songs, sweet as dew
Muse to me Thou art, o Herald bold
No voice is clearer, no speech more compelling than
Thine
I am moved to motion by Thee,
my spirit kindled by Thy call!
The hot spark of Thy feathers among the heavens,
Thy home,
pours light upon mine eyes
The gentle mists that flow from Thy sea-swept
          pitcher
pour life into my body
How gladdened am I by Thee, o Iris!
My lungs revel in Thy breath, my skin in Thy
          wingbeats
My heart glides with Thee, dear Wife of Winds,
o Daughter of Sea and Cloud
I dance in Thy rains, dance in Thy bright rays,
dance beside Thy kin in the graceful waves,
dance beneath Thy kin in the jubilant skies

My energies are Thine, Mistress of the Spectrum
My heart and my words, my songs are Thine
My ears are Thine, my power is Thine
if Thy power may be mine as well
Let me share in Thy experience
Let me carry Thy burdens, Thy joys,
as mine are carried by Thee, Handmaiden Goddess
Let me bear Thy peace as mine is borne by Thee
Let me inspire Thee as I am inspired by Thee,
        o Iris!

May I be the prism of Thy light,
the mirror to Thy sweet soul
May my service by Thine, as Thy service is to
        Olympos
Our service to the Gods and the Worlds, o Goddess
        fearless!
May the Winds be devoted to Thee
as Thou art devoted to all,
as I am devoted to Thee, Glory of the Queen of a
        thousand Eyes
Let Thy purpose be mine
as the purpose of the Horizon King is Thine

Hail Iris, the Messenger, the Rainbow!
Praised Thou art! Praise be to Thee!

How Hermes Got His Wings

by Melia Brokaw

A woman frantically spins a crystal in the light from the window making rainbows swirl around the room. "Iris, storm-footed and golden winged, you who nursed my child when I could not, hear me. My boy has been taken from his cradle by Apollon, furious to behold. Tell his father! Bring my baby back!"

Iris takes Maia's message to Zeus. She just barely beats Apollon back to the hall. Zeus bids her to wait in an ante chamber while he deals with the problem. As she leaves, Iris sees a very angry Apollon dragging her milk-child by his swaddling clothes. The clothes have tangled around his legs which is the only thing keeping Hermes from escaping. Meanwhile, the child's arms are flailing about trying to find purchase on something in order to pull himself out of his angry half-brother's grasp. She hurries out before her laughter can anger the far-darter even more. She hears Apollon shout, "He's stolen my cattle! Then he has the temerity to kill one in the name of the Olympians!"

Her amusement was short lived however. Here she was cooling her heels when she had a long scroll worth of duties that needed to be done before Helios was done for the day. "So many gods and only one of me!" Iris thought. Occasionally she could hear Apollon's musical tenor and Hermes' high pitched reply followed by the low pitches of Zeus. Muttering she started pacing in circles, causing a tight rainbow corkscrew that was taking her perilously close to the ceiling.

Suddenly she heard a "Now son and no more of your lip!" After they left, Zeus bade Iris return to the hall. With a sigh and a wave of the hand, her colorful trail slowly dissolved allowing her to return to the floor.

When she returned to the foot of Zeus' throne, she found Zeus with his brows furrowed in thought. "My lord?"

"Oh that child is a scamp! He's going to need to be kept busy and sooner than I thought. So much energy! So much zeal for mischief!"

*Listening to the head of the pantheon ponder was **not** on her list of things to get done today*, she thought to herself. While Zeus thought out loud, Iris proceeded to silently try to figure out ways to cut out lag time so at least the super important things got done. Then figure out *who* she could risk angering when she put off their messages until tomorrow. The clearing of a throat broke her out of her reverie.

"Oh! I'm sorry my lord!"

"Busy day?" he asks.

"Yes, sir. There are so many of us now and only one of me."

"As I was saying, Hermes needs an occupation. Something that will keep him moving and expend his energies in a useful fashion, otherwise only more trouble will follow. That is where you come in."

"Me? You mean … oh yes. Yes! I can think of no one better to help me! Acting as messenger will keep him busy enough that his tendency to mischievousness will be limited."

"As his wet nurse, he's used to minding you, so there should be minimal problems with training. He is plenty smart so the training shouldn't take long anyway."

"Well, as well as he minds anyone, excepting you. I think your son will make a perfect messenger for you."

"Me?"

"Yes, sir. The acorn didn't fall far from the oak, sir. He came by his mischievousness honestly and will, therefore, be much better suited to your needs than I am." Privately, she was more than elated by this solution. It will free her up for her own pursuits and allow her to truthfully claim ignorance to the Queen when her husband committed some misdeed.

Zeus eyed the colorful messenger thoughtfully. She had the uncomfortable feeling that he knew exactly what she was thinking. "Well. Make the arrangements … tomorrow. I've delayed your other duties long enough today."

"Yes, sir. Thank you, sir." Iris however was no longer paying the King of the Gods any heed. She left the hall to continue with her duties … after one short unplanned stop, Hephaistos' forge. I've been wanting a new pair of wings. Something prettier, more colorful than these golden ones. I'll give these to Hermes and ask Hephaistos for something smaller, lighter and more in keeping with my rainbow trail. Something like Zephyr's wings. Won't he like that!"

Epithets of Iris

by Rachel Petersen

Storm-footed Iris of the arching rainbow
Daughter of wondrous seas and shining clouds
Favored wife of kind, bold Zephyros
Gentle handmaiden of the crowns of Olympos
Ambassador of Zeus, lightning thrower and king of
      the powers above
and of Hera, confident queen and granter of bliss in
      marriage and home
Messenger swift and oathkeeper fair
Loyal watcher of the skies and follower of storms
Waker of dreams by thunder's command
Bringer of waters that bind the gods' pledges
Peaceful golden-winged beauty and angel of the
      Olympians
Faithful guardian and carrier of blessings
Bright keeper of colors and rain Goddess generous
Balance of duty and pleasure, of service and pride
Bridge of heaven and earth and of all worlds
Sacred, radiant muse and speaker of trusted words
Woman of humble light and gemstone brilliance
Glory of sunshine on waves, glitter of morning dew,
and fireglow in evening smoke
Shimmer of songbird feathers, beetle shells,
dragonfly lenses, and butterfly capes
Inspiration to the heart and voice in all seasons
Lovely spirit who calls the artist's soul to flight

The Rainbow

by Callum Hurley

Thunk.

Gabriel accepted his passport dis-
passionately back from the unsmiling customs
officer, and ambled forward without a word. The
mood in an immigration line could never be
described as particularly bright, but today he could
almost feel his own dejection seeping outwards and
smothering it even beyond the norm. As he walked
through the metal gate his feet seemed to barely
clear the dirty, carpeted floor, giving the unsettling
impression of a shade gliding sadly through the
sterile space. His face was drawn, lined and
bearded, looking so unlike the youthful visage in his
passport that he was once again almost surprised to
not be detained. But it wasn't simply the hair and
other accumulated marks of neglect that
transformed him, but that undefinable something
born of months and months of pain and loneliness.
He felt the familiar pang in his chest when catching
a glance at the photograph as he folded the
document and tucked it away in his pocket; he
simply did not recognise the man within it. A face
so like his own gazed back at him, but in it was a
man who had lived in a different world entirely to
the one his feet trudged reluctantly through now.

He continued his journey along the tape-
lined hallway in silence. Each step was a weary

affair, his humble hand luggage seeming to impose a force far beyond it's actual stature. He was vaguely aware of the crowds swiftly passing him by, all in the conventional human rush to get where they needed to be right away. Beside him a family of four powered past him, the parents clearly striding to keep pace with their excited children. Gabriel couldn't help but feel a fleeting note of hostility at this, he had once been where he wanted to be too, and now there was nowhere else to go. He felt the familiar jolt in his mind, the familiar flutter in his chest, that foretold a long, unpleasant night of hurt and fruitless, self-destructive attempts to resist it.

His head still pounded from the night before, and he had honestly hoped to avoid drinking at all tonight if he could. That self deception was as empty now as it had always been, and was slipping quickly into it's daily, inevitable phase of clarity. Why must he repeat this same fucking process every day? It was maddening. Quickly he engaged his particular, well-practiced procedure of composure, the voices of various therapists and wise men ringing across his mind in a muddle. As always a cacophony of emotion swirled biliously within him, but Gabriel struggled hard to keep the currents from condensing into corporeal thoughts. Empty the mind, let the thoughts pass, he had heard these words from every half-baked doctor and repeated them endlessly ever since. It never worked of course, but he somehow felt he still got credit for trying (though from whom he wasn't exactly sure). Whilst he successfully resisted words there was no resisting the memory of that goddam photograph, which had managed to imprint itself behind his eyelids and adamantly refused to budge.

He recalled vividly the day that particular photography had been taken, and once again he found his tired, disobedient mind drifting back into it.

At the time it had seemed merely a overlooked chore, drowned out by the volume of tasks competing for attention. It had been an exhausting morning, hectic and full of feigned opinions and cheery failed attempts to seem interested. Gabe's good friend had once told him that he swore that all wedding dresses were in fact absolutely identical, with only an elaborate conspiracy tasked at convincing the women of the world that they, in fact, had a decision to make. That good friend was now Gabe's best man, and as they sat together outside of a changing room a wordless confirmation of that theory passed between them. And if wedding dresses were indeed identical he wasn't sure what that made of china patterns, which must consequently have been duplicates at a molecular level.

But to Gabe these concerns seemed to pass as chaff in the wind, who in his happy delirium barely seemed to register the specifics. After the shopping was complete, and with a collection of military standard issue dresses and china in tow, the small party had congregated in a department store restaurant for a late lunch. The meal itself was unremarkable, but a wonderful atmosphere pervaded the humble, unplanned affair. Free of the regiments of organisation and planning he at last felt fully comfortable, and it felt as though the very spirit of the world responded in kind. Everyone he thought can recall at least one such social occasion, one time when the stars just seemed to simply align and everyone had the most enjoyable time owed to nothing but themselves. Good cheer (aided by perhaps a little too much daytime champagne) flowed easily, the best man and maid of honour speeches were roughly brainstormed and embarrassing stories shook the restaurant with laughter.

Gabriel was a man never settled in one place, perhaps having lived in four different countries throughout his childhood had contributed to this, and no matter how satisfied he became with a situation he always felt the most frustrating itch to move on to another. Indeed, when he had first announced his intent to marry it had been met with a general, poorly-concealed surprise on the part of his friends and family, who it quickly became clear had never expected such a thing of him.

But right there, then, he had felt a permeating lack of inclination to be anywhere else at all. The feeling was so novel, so conspicuous, that it had imprinted itself in his head like a flashbulb. In truth he could recall little of the details of that meal, most of the conversation had faded in his recollection, and he recalled only some vague manner of fancy sandwich on his plate, the details so incidental that he had not even bothered to remember them. But that feeling, the 'rightness', that had never left him.

Too soon the plates were cleared and glasses drained, and the party began to gather itself to head homeward. It was at this point that he was reminded by her that his passport needed renewing for the honeymoon, and that they the store had a photo-booth that they could drop whilst they were here. After brief explanations were offered to the diffused party it was quickly established that the others would go on ahead, and that she and Gabriel would stay behind and catch up with them later on. A murmur of 'goodbyes', hugs, and kissed cheeks duly followed, and they parted ways at the door, the gaggle of siblings, friends and cousins going one way, and he another, her hand within his.

Her. River.

Gabriel was jolted back into reality by the stinging sensation in his eye. How much her very name stung him so, like warm water on a open sore. He hadn't realised that he had been avoiding thinking it until that very moment, and almost immediately her presence popped into every memory he still held in his mind. River modelling her chosen dress for him at the changing room, River's bright smile as she confidently proclaimed their china pattern as 'the one', River's musical laugh at lunch, River's soft fingers within his, and finally River's eyes meeting his as she organised yet another small, disjointed, forgotten part of his life.

River.

He hissed a curse as a betraying tear grew defiantly in the corner of his right eye. In his trance he had somehow reached the baggage claim, and he could feel the eyes of his fellow passengers hot within his cheeks. He wanted to tell himself that nobody had noticed, but he knew that they almost certainly had. So imposingly ragged was his figure that he drew constant stares these days, his every expression at the scrutiny of the unknowing masses. What they thought of him he wasn't exactly sure, but he had a fair idea, and often tortured himself with speculation. Drug dealer, vagrant, common thief, in truth he knew he looked like some combination all of the down-and-out aspects of society.

Signs written in Thai indicated which carousels were which, requiring Gabriel to reluctantly follow the excitable family to know which was his, necessitating a light jog to avoid losing the children's miniature frames in the meandering crowd. They had been sitting across the aisle from him throughout the entire flight, he recognised this once he was stood beside them impatiently awaiting his tattered bag, but he could have sworn not to notice them before customs. Was this another memory that his mind had surreptitiously neglected to provide him? How much of his life was now lost this way he wondered, diffused into mindless disattention? He wanted to care, wanted to be appalled by the notion, but the feeling just wouldn't rise within him. He felt half-alive, and couldn't muster the energy to object.

As he hailed a cab he prepared for the same old conflict with the language barrier that had irritated him for months. Once again the excitable family were to be found nearby mirroring him, with the parents visibly struggling to juggle loading luggage and bundling their children into the waiting taxi, mindful no doubt of the impatient line of eager drivers behind them. They appeared harried, and Gabriel wondered where and to what end they were headed, and whether they too might look upon him with the same envy as he did they. If so they were fools, his pain was of a different breed to whatever beset them, lucky people so rarely recognised themselves as such in his experience.

Before long his turn had arrived, and after a series of vague expressions and long stares at a map the car pulled away from the kerb, beginning it's frantic, dangerous journey to the destination. Gabriel had been fully expecting this, it had been much the same in Cambodia and Vietnam, and as such he sat with an amount of disinterest that astonished even him. The taxi drove into oncoming traffic, tore through car parks and mounted kerbs with abandon, and Gabriel did wonder absent mindedly if this might once again be the last leg of his long, long journey. When in Vietnam he had once asked a local lady about why the people drove with such dangerous disregard, and had received a casual answer that had stuck with him ever since. "It's nice", she had said (in thick broken English), "to get up in a morning and not know if you'll be back there in the night". It had resonated with him immediately, the thought of an end to life often felt like only thing that kept him going.

The heat in the car was terribly stifling, making the already not insignificant journey feel long and exhausting. He could clearly tell that the point of no return had passed, the night was not going to be a pleasant affair and he made no further effort to delude himself to the contrary. River's image and words now criss-crossed unhindered across his mind, and he surrendered himself to them gladly. This form of memory was the worst kind of addiction, one that he knew would inevitably make him suffer, but that provided him with a catharsis that he could not elsewhere find.

That photograph had not entered into his life alone. Once, it had been a twin. The booth in the department store had been that rare thing, a forgiving machine, offering two copies each of three separate attempts, with a kindly series of instructions with regards to which to choose for use for official documents. Gabe remembered smiling at this, feeling a gratitude to this inanimate object that even at the time he knew was silly. But it just seemed so nice, so humble and welcoming, just a little way in which somebody was trying their best to make life a little easier. He had shared this thought with River and recalled her tinkling laugh as clearly as if she were sat there in that cab with him. She had accused him of being in danger of becoming a cheerful man, and he had agreed that they should remain vigilant against such a frightful possibility. The love that he had felt for her there was so powerful that it reverberated undiminished across the time and space separating this moment from that, with such an intensity that Gabriel was sure the Driver would notice it.

The first attempt had been a pure disaster. Gabe's head was too big, too wonky and his face was drawn into an involuntary smile of self-consciousness and embarrassment. That photograph was lost unceremoniously to the annals of history. As the little counter on screen counted down he steeled himself for the second attempt (mindful of the fact that he did not have enough change for another go around), expecting to get a little closer this time in preparation for the successful third try. To his surprise and satisfaction, he nailed it on the second try. This would later go on to become one of the crowning victories of his entire existence.

With his passport photograph secure he had moved to exit the booth, abandoning his third attempt to a photograph of the blank white backdrop. But before he had a chance to move River had swept into the booth like a fresh breeze, congratulated him upon a job well done, and planted a playful kiss upon him just as the flash fired. Everything about that kiss, that perfect moment of perfect spontaneity, was somehow frozen into a piece of celluloid and offered to him as a gift as they exited the booth. They had immediately loved that photograph, taking a copy each later that very day, as the day's plunder was cut with scissors and attached to various pieces of paper.

There were many photographs taken on the day of the wedding, rare and graceful things replete with flowing (identical) white dresses and classy fixtures. He was plenty fond of them all, indeed one had hung proudly upon the wall of their short lived Edinburgh home. But no photograph before or since could compare with the one tucked away into his wallet, the one that greeted him every time he bought a cup of coffee, or checked the account number of his bank card for the hundredth time that day. That moment, that simple, heraldless moment, had been the happiest of his life and now he could carry it with him forever.

River.

He had burnt it.

One night in Fiji, he had been staying at a resort on a tiny island. The hour was late, he had known not when, but there and been no sight or hint of the Sun for many hours, since long after he and taken his first drink. He had not known why he had to visit Fiji and all attempts at an explanation had failed, just that he must and no reason or counsel could dissuade him. Fiji had been the destination of a honeymoon that had never come, and he felt that the country owed him something personally, owed him a happiness that had been promised but never delivered. Gabriel was told repeatedly that he walked through a paradise, but he saw nothing but emptiness, but heat and water and insects and the thankless sun. As he laid there, beside the crackling flames, he had truthfully and earnestly wanted to die.

This had seemed like a good place for him to die, he had followed River as far as he was able and now had only one way to follow her further. And as he coughed and swallowed another shot of tasteless liquor he had hoped that he would not awaken in the morning. This beach was miles away from anywhere he reasoned, nobody would be able to 'save' him in time, nobody would be able to force him back to a World he no longer had a place in. What a perfect end to his story it would have made, a cowardly, wretched end to contrast with that of his brave, kind, beloved wife.

He had been more drunk that night than he ever thought it was possible to be and survive. And as he had stared upon the photograph, a photograph that he knew so well that it was unnecessary to even remove it from his wallet on most occasions, the pain and hatred had welled up within him until he was helpless before it. Nothing had been worth this suffering, this anguish, he so hated this world, his life and everything about all of it. And he cast the photograph into the merciless flame, seeking finally to be rid of himself, all of his cursed memories, at last. He subsequently credited only passing out drunk for having spared him from joining it.

In the morning he discovered his previous naivety, he was capable of hating something even more than his fate: himself. He wailed and screamed with such fury that it seemed to the other guests upon the island that a wild animal had infiltrated their little haven. He had punched and punched the furniture of his room until his knuckles were unrecognisable, he had head-butted the mirror with such force that it had shattered so that his head bled profusely, coating the quaint shack with bright, red, acrid blood. His memories became fuzzy after that, but he recalled well the rocking of the small boat that took him to a hospital syncing in time with his own. The scars were set upon his face still, transforming him irrevocably from the happy, victorious man that lived in his passport, in his past. But in truth the scars that the glass left meant less than nothing to him, only material, only fleeting, painless. The scars of River's death, of his great, epic loss, they burned and burned and never for a moment stopped burning.

He cried, silent and still. The driver, preoccupied with a combination of trying not to die and making it as likely as possible, was obviously unaware. He loved her so very much, River. She had been perfect, soft without being gullible, strong without being harsh. He had lost his certainty of many things in the past months, but he knew this memory was clear and reliable and unaffected by time. Such people only existed in soppy stories, in tragic love tales and romantic comedies, people so wonderful and human that you could scarcely believe that they exist. And River had been very human, sometimes snappy, sometimes jealous, and sometimes sad. At one point she had even left him for a little while, requiring time to overcome her uncertainty before she returned. But this was what made her perfect to him, she represented the very best that a human, saddled with our cruel condition and the harshness of the World, could ever be expected to be. She had been kind and caring and she had loved him in a way that he had never deserved. And he had repaid her by burning the last evidence he still had of their time together to appease his own selfish pain. He hated himself, truly, deeply, wordlessly.

Before long the car turned along a narrow side road and approached the beachside resort. Lost in memory the journey's character had furtively shifted, the latter stages having passed in a timeless blur. Gabriel tried and struggled to recall the scenery after the car had left the city, but was rewarded with very little. Pulling up before the door he stepped out of the car and handed the Driver a large colourful bank note, not even bothering to check the value or expect change. River's corporate life insurance policy had eliminated any and all financial concerns, and Gabriel didn't exactly have long term plans for the money. Appropriately the

Driver did not query further, getting back in the Driver's seat and pulling away quickly, only narrowing avoiding killing a stray cat in the process.

Gabriel stepped through the door and conducted the tedious check-in process that he had been through a thousand times, finally strolling along the path and into his wooden cabin. The first sight that actually registered in his mind was that of a large double bed, a standard feature in almost every place that Gabriel had stayed, few people, after all, travel alone. It never ceased to pain him, and he could already tell that this was one of those nights that he wouldn't be sleeping in it. Alcohol would ensure that he would lay wherever it was that he eventually found himself.

Her death had been swift and brutal. By the time cancer was discovered it was already far too late and widespread to treat, and River had unanimously refused the various futile attempts offered to her. The red flag had first been raised when they had visited the doctor for a travel vaccination followup, only eight weeks before they were due to depart on the honeymoon. By the time that day arrived, River was gone. They had initially wanted to leave directly after the wedding, but were convinced to delay in order to save money for the trip. River had been excited about learning to SCUBA dive, and Gabe was calling in every debt to make it a possibility, scrimping, borrowing, the wedding having taken a large toll upon the couples finances.

Concerned that the injections were making her ill, the Doctor had elected to investigate further. They had returned home together that evening, eaten dinner and fallen asleep early in each others arms. The very next day River was told that she had only weeks to live. Gabriel's stomach knotted as he thought back upon that night and how nondescript and forgettable it had been. If there had been any notion at all that it would be the last happy, carefree evening they would spend together, if only he had known, the things they would have done, he should have remembered every second, never allowed it to end. After returning form the oncologist that evening they laid together in their humble double bed for countless hours, Gabriel in tears whilst River simply clung to him, blank and silent in a way he had never known her to be. He felt her, so warm and alive, and simply could not comprehend that she would soon be cold and lifeless. Everything about her then was burned into his memory like a still sore brand, the lost luster of her bright red hair in the grey dark, her beautiful face transformed into an empty and terrified mask. He kissed her constantly, it seemed to be the only outside stimulus of she was aware, and she responded obediently in kind each and every time. He had no words to offer her, could think of nothing to at all to say, and after a few initial attempts at verbal comfort he simply lay there, holding her, in silence.

She suffered beautifully, despite her cruel, terrible pain, never losing the undefinable essence of what made her his beloved, of what made her, her. As she declined the World declined with her, becoming cold and meaningless. The light of the Sun lost all warmth, the World became nothing but a half-forgotten dream upon waking from her. She never once failed to return his kiss, not a single time, even at the last as her life support were disconnected and she faded into nothingness before his very eyes. The very last movement she would ever make was her lips coming together and gently brushing his.

The sky began to darken outside, and Gabriel was eventually coaxed out by the unmistakable sound of revelry upon the beach below. As was so often the case he sought simply to forget the World, uncaring of where he was or why. He had no love or particular appreciation of this country, it was simply another place to wander to, another place that wasn't where he was before. Part of him acknowledged the futility of trying to outrun his pain, just as he knew so clearly the morning after he had burnt the photograph. But it was the one thing that he could do, and keep doing, to give him some distraction, the world was enormous and he knew he wouldn't run out of places to wander to in whatever remained of his life.

The beach below was crowded with people and fires, sprinkled liberally across it's length in small aggregations. Gabriel had heard much about such events from others on his travels, 'Full Moon Parties' they were called, and they were everywhere in Thailand. Once he had ridden on a bus for hours, overhearing a group of friends loudly discussing their conquests and drug induced experiences at the events, to the annoyance of both himself and his fellow passengers. Certainly he was in no spirits for a party, but the beach was warm and comfortable and a better alternative to his lonely, darkened cabin. He walked down to the sands and promptly accepted a large bucket of some kind of cocktail from an excitable young Thai woman in a bikini, paying with an offhanded wad of cash. The concoction was sweet and acidic, with a taste that he couldn't even begin to place, but it was clearly potent and Gabriel cared about little else. He took a long swig and laid against a curved tree, waiting impatiently for the alcohol to dull his senses, and thus his pain.

He didn't have to wait long, and began to feel the familiar light-headedness almost immediately. Every part of his body seemed to quickly thank him at once for the drink, his head softened, his shoulders relaxed, and his stomach eased, and it occurred to him once again that his obvious addiction was continuing to worsen. His lack of concern about this surprised him less than the danger of the cab ride had, indeed he had long ago given up the pretence that he had any concern for his wellbeing beyond that which raw instinct imposed. This particular method of self-destruction and he had long been cordial by this stage. People continually passed here and there, some tried to speak to him, but he dismissed them with the fewest words he could manage. As always he wanted only to be alone, since the loss of River he felt that nobody else could possibly begin to understand him now, others felt like foreign beings with whom he shared very little.

By the time he had drained the bucket he was drunk in earnest, and felt like an outsider observing the world as opposed to part of it. He looked down and saw a disgusting, ruined man, for whom he felt nothing but pity and revulsion, but the drink shielded him having to care. In a short order he had bought another and continued to drink, his tired body being too practiced at eliminating the alcohol from his system, almost as though it too wanted him to feel, to suffer.

For hours he sat in stupor whilst the World moved loudly around him, music blared and harsh, splitting laughter reverberated endlessly. As always he eventually lost track of how much he had drunk, and just continued to do so heedlessly for the duration. Time passed into the familiar nothing, wherein hours of thoughtlessness seemed as minutes, and those minutes of thinking upon his past seemed as hours. For how long he lay there he could not say, but groups of people came and left without his ever having moved. Twice he staggered to his feet, stumbled to the rocks bordering the sea and took a piss. On one of those occasions he also vomited a grotesque multi-coloured substance that mixed in a disgusting manner with the seawater below. But beyond this he did nothing but languish, sinking mind and body into the warm sands.

He became steadily aware that he was something of a novelty to the other partygoers, who variously unsubtly commented on him and reacted with a diverse mixture of amusement and disgust. Their words couldn't reach him at all in this state, he was far beyond the petty concerns that drove the naive people that surrounded him. River was dead, she was dead and gone and she was never coming back. Nothing else mattered now, not a goddam fucking thing. His reason for being had passed, he was simply waiting to follow, too cowardly to take his own life and join her.

After an undefinable amount of time it rather suddenly begun to rain, and rain hard indeed. The party quickly broke apart and scattered, the few remaining partygoers by this point presumably retreating back into their respective rooms. But Gabriel didn't move an inch, he wasn't sure that he even could and felt no imputes to try. Once more his desire to move had been defeated, a dark reflection of that fateful day. The rain washed over him in torrents, but could not clean the scars from his face, nor could it touch the scars within. Alone at last he slowly drifted into an unconscious awakeness, utterly unable to find true rest. Gradually, slowly, the sun began to claw at the horizon and the littered, party-scarred form of his surroundings crept gradually into view.

And it was there, as clearly as a hand before his face, that he saw her.

River.

Or so he initially thought. Every fibre of his being had sobered instantly at the sight, his faculties rushing back behind his eyes like a crashing wave. As they did Gabriel quickly realised that it clearly wasn't her, but his blood still buzzed electrically with the excitement of the lingering moment. He had dreamed of her of course, vividly and often, and the feeling that filled him now mirrored that sensation almost exactly. In an instant the tenor of the World shifted, as though a switch had been flicked, and the light of the raising sun briefly blinded him as he squinted his eyes to inspect her more closely. This woman did indeed bare an uncanny resemblance to River, but, astonishingly, this instantly became amongst the least notable aspects of her appearance.

The figure before him radiated with a continually shifting light of every colour, it seemed that by the time his eyes managed to focus in upon one tone another had taken it's place. Gabriel's first indication that this was not simply a bizarre trick of the morning light meeting his drunken faculties came when his gaze caught her feet. Where they lay upon the beach before him they left no imprint at all in the sand, somehow this 'woman' imparted no weight upon the ground below. Even with his mind working with electrical efficiency it took Gabriel a long moment to process this, the whole while staring dumbly at the ground, as though he might catch it behaving properly if he were only vigilant enough. After confirming that this was not going to happen his gaze crawled back to her face, and the air around him became thick and difficult to inhale. Her physical beauty was breathtaking, astonishingly so, to the extent that Gabriel soon felt compelled to avert his gaze for reasons he could not logically reason. He felt like a deer trapped in the headlights of an oncoming truck, stunned and too bemused to react.

He immediately made a mental move to remain calm, reminding himself that he had experienced similar things once before. In South America, whilst staying in a rather rundown hostel, he had taken LSD, and had the most extreme night of his entire life, beset by vivid and unpleasant hallucinations wherever he looked. He had spoken to other angry versions of himself, heard the malicious voices of friends long passed and felt the presence of strange creatures watching and pursuing him. Worst of all, he had seen the weeping image of a cancer-striken River moving constantly beyond his grasp, just as the end of a rainbow retreats from the observer. In the end he had curled into a ball and placed his fingers in his ears, screaming to cover the imagined bustle. It had not been an experience he had been keen to repeat, and he was not sure how it was now happening again. Regaining his composure his thoughts turned to the drinks, somebody must have spiked one of the myriad buckets of disgusting liquor that he had consumed throughout the long evening. There was no way he would have noticed whilst that drunk, and whilst consuming something with a taste so surreal.

That must be it, some asshole on this beach must have snuck a hallucinogenic in his drink, and now he was hallucinating. Yet this felt very different from his previous experience with LSD, and he began examining the situation comparatively in his mind. Before there had been a host of hallucinations and voices, but a quick circular glance confirmed to him that the glowing figure was alone amongst the surroundings that he knew to be real. Indeed, last time, parts of the environment itself had also moved and behaved strangely, he recalled the terrifying sensation of the floor beneath his feet sinking beneath his feet and shivered slightly, but here the rest of the dirty beach remained stubbornly unremarkable. Overwhelmingly though there was just the feeling, it felt very, very different. Last time he had been terrified, truly horrified to the extent that he had fought with the thought that he had finally died and slipped into Hell for his behaviour. It had taken the most ardent effort simply to recall basic information such as who and where he was. But now he felt totally himself and no longer the least bit drunk, filled with an odd sense of peace and security. He didn't feel threatened by this figure, whatever it was, and this confused him, as he felt honestly that he really should. Perhaps it hadn't been LSD he reasoned, but another hallucinogenic substance with different effects.

He turned his gaze back to the figure, who, during the entire period that he had been pursuing this train of thought, hadn't moved at all. And by this he meant literally, the figure stood, or rather floated, with an unnatural stillness that no human could ever replicate. Her gaze was fixed squarely upon him, and as their eyes met he could feel someone else staring into him just as intelligently as he did in return. It, 'She' he supposed he should say, apparently wasn't going anywhere, and he wasn't really sure what to do with her. The Englishman in him couldn't help but rankle slightly at the rudeness of simply leaving her standing there, and this thought was so absurd that he genuinely almost laughed aloud, surprising himself. After a long self-conscious moment, during which he chastised himself several times for being ridiculous, and a solid minute or more after first noticing her, he finally, quiveringly spoke:

"Err…hello?"

"Gabriel Vance," she gently replied.

Her voice quivered with energy, as though the sound infused the very air it touched with excitement. It was lilting and warm, and no sooner had the last tone faded away than Gabriel found himself somehow missing it. He was almost surprised to see her face move as she spoke, it was the very first movement of any kind that she had

104

performed since her appearance. Most stunningly of all her face curved into a warm smile as the lips closed, and Gabriel could scarcely believe that something so incredible could come from within his imagination. She appeared human only as a great work of art does, bearing the basic form of the subject but more beautiful and crafted than any natural thing.

After a second or two she spoke again. "I am Iris, of the Rainbow", she continued, naturally enough, "and I am sent with a message".

She spoke this with a stable tone that longed to imply that it was unremarkable enough, but Gabriel didn't bother attempting to suppress his befuddlement. He knew that name well, Iris was a Greek Goddess and he did not require, nor ask, for any explanation beyond that simple introduction. Indeed, he learned everything there was to know about her in the very class at University where he and River had first met. What a bizarre thing this was for him to dream up now, he couldn't recall thinking about her again after that exam paper was closed over four years ago. Why on Earth was she now back in his mind?

"A message," he said back.

It was not a question, he knew well that Iris was a messenger of the Gods and that made a notion of sense.

"From whom?"

He wasn't entirely sure exactly why he was playing along like this, but as he had come this far he felt he should see this through to it's conclusion. The beach had been cleared by the rain, nobody was there to see the spectacle of this surreal episode anyway.

"From River," she answered simply.

The effect those two words had upon him threatened to completely revolve the entire melancholy mood that had prevailed thus far. A host of emotions swept through him in an instant, sorrow, longing, and finally anger. He looked the figure straight in the eye.

"Oh fuck off," he stated plainly, "I don't need this shit, I get enough of this everyday anyway. Could you please, honestly just fuck the hell off."

As was often the case he was angry at his mind for devising another, admittedly original, way to torture him and he wanted it to know so. If this thing was a hallucination it was as though he was speaking directly to his subconscious, and whilst his voice wasn't raised he held back none of the malice in his words. The figure didn't appear the least bit surprised by this sudden burst of hostility, indeed it appeared from her almost amused expression that it had been exactly what she had expected.

"She warned me you might say something like that." She replied, Gabriel hadn't been sure that she would, with something that was recognisably a laugh. It was musical, resonant, unlike any laugh Gabriel had ever imagined. Gabriel turned away and she didn't press the matter, remaining silent until he turned back and looked at her again.

"Would you like to hear the message?"

Gabriel scoffed and slapped the sand beneath him in frustration, buffering some up into his face and stinging his eyes. What exactly had he done to deserve this kind of crap yet again, why did it seem to single him out and follow him so fervently. It was enough to drive a man to despair. But despite himself, perhaps it was simply the long sleepless night that had left him feeling weary and resigned, he couldn't fully suppress his curiosity. Whatever madness it was this time it could hardly make it any worse.

"Sure," he sighed eventually, and with a hint of poorly concealed factiousness, "why not."

Iris smiled at this, and he once again couldn't resist the feeling of security that followed. It was unmistakable that this hallucination, whatever it was, clearly had no ill intention toward him. Despite himself yet again he felt his hostility melting away in lieu of his best attempts to preserve it, slipping through his fingers like the residual grains of sand in his palm.

"River sends you her love Gabriel," she said, "she sends you her love from beyond this fleeting world."

Gabriel's eyes remained fixed on her throughout the time it took to speak this sentence, but they dropped back down to the sand when Iris finished speaking. He replied, this time without meeting her gaze,

"I see, well that's very nice indeed, but I am a little disappointed that I couldn't come up with anything a little more elaborate than that I have to say."

He raised his eye to look at her agin and she smiled, with amusement but plainly, once again, not surprise.

"Although, it is nice to see my mind at least making an effort to help for once," he sighed and felt his shoulders sink. "I guess that's something . ..." He was exhausted, physically as much as emotionally, and couldn't muster the energy to get worked up about this again. He knew it would pass soon enough, he might as well just roll with it.

Iris looked at him curiously, and Gabriel could see something far more human begin to creep into her flawless visage. A kindness bloomed in her features, she looked at him as though he had moved from being the recipient of a message, a client if you will, to something else. It almost seemed that she could relax and open up now that her job was done, and the gesture was so human, so fallible, that for the first time Gabriel truly felt that he were speaking to another independent being. This sensation struck him with such an erie certainty that he couldn't stop himself from asking her:

"What are you really? Are you an hallucination?"

"Perhaps I am," Iris seemed to muse, "but what is the World but a hallucination after all."

Gabriel just looked at her blankly, he certainly wasn't in the mood for philosophy, so she continued:

"Most importantly though does it really matter? My message to you remains the same."

Gabriel felt that he must have a dozen retorts to such an absurd comment, but none would quite form properly on the tongue. He was beginning to become more and more bewildered as this conversation (for lack of a better term) progressed, he could not fathom how this surreal episode could be being played out by his own mind. Most of all the mention of River was eroding away at his logical faculties, and he could quickly feel himself being drawn into a sinking emotional reasoning, whereby he didn't particularly care about the specifics of what was happening just as Iris suggested.

"It kind of matters to me though," he eventually managed to reply. "I have more memories and dreams about River than I know what to do with but a real message from beyond, well that would be a new one on me."

Gabriel had though about life after death surprisingly little for someone who's entire life had recently been dictated and destroyed by it. He had always believed in something, a kind of oneness, but had never dared to attempt to rationalise or reason what that all meant. He cared so little for his own life these days that he didn't fear death at all, and he thought that took away a large part of the imputes that usually drives people to struggle for the answers. He just hoped that he would find River again in whatever form, that was all that mattered to him.

Iris actually seemed to consider this for a little while before speaking:

"Rest assured that it is real enough by your criteria Gabriel Vance, and that whatever I may be that the message is from her and not of yourself. I am with you both, both here and there, now and before. Forgive me if I confuse you but things appear very differently to us, it is sometimes difficult for us to relate to distinctions as you do."

Gabriel was once again electrified by this small monologue, it touched upon philosophical arguments that he had once had with himself and never fully managed to refute in either direction. It began to occur to him, in some wild, ridiculous corner of his mid that this might be a real religious experience of some kind. The implications of this notion shocked him to his very core. He was compelled, irrevocably now, to ask further.

"Are you saying that you don't see things as being separate?"

"No," Iris replied after a short pause. Gabriel could have sworn that her brow briefly furrowed, as though she were struggling to focus upon something distant. "Less separate than you though perhaps. The more that you can see the less separate things appear to be."

"Is this real?" he asked again. He knew that he was labouring this point, but he couldn't help it,;this whole event was so outlandish on every level that he was struggling to comprehend it at all.

"Yes, Gabriel I am," Iris replied more confidently and without hesitation this time. "I have been called by many names and taken many forms in many lives. I remember many things. These things I do believe make me real, as you would describe it. And I am here to deliver you a message, as I have always done."

Gabriel's mouth was so dry that he found it difficult to reply. With those words everything about his surroundings, and place within them, seemed to have somehow changed without changing at all.

"River." That was all he could eventually make able to say.

"She loves you so very much, Gabriel." Iris spoke now without being prompted. He could feel a social wall between them being broken down, as though the ice had been broken. "She is part of me and I am part of that love too now and it is the realest thing. More real than here or there, or life or death."

Gabriel began to gently cry, he couldn't help it. He still had no idea if this was all bullshit or not, but something about Iris's words seemed to move him regardless. It didn't seem to matter where they came from, their effect upon him was the same. Iris smiled at him and leant forward, so that Gabriel for a moment thought she was going to move towards him. But at the last second she stood back to her full hight, a sense of formality renewed, and continued to speak.

"She says that sending me here is the last time that she can help you Gabriel, that you must live for her too now and that this, what you're doing now, isn't right. She sends me with a promise, a promise that she is with you and part of you always. And in return you must promise to live as though she were you too, and do for yourself as you would do for her."

Gabriel was overwhelmed by these words, totally, absolutely overwhelmed, and for minutes could not speak or react. The weight of their implication seemed to dominate his entire mental capacity and capability to feel, so that there was simply nothing left over. After a long time, during which time Iris waited without the slightest hint of impatience in her motionless posture, Gabriel asked simply,

"Where is she?"

"I couldn't say, Gabriel, I don't really know either …," Iris said, and every hint of the formality of a moment ago had once again vanished completely, "…but she is there, and she is here, too. That much I can see for myself. By the stories of the people who name I gave you could say that she is in the Underworld, in Elysium, that she is at peace at Persephone's table. All I can tell you is that by asking the question you are already outside of the answer, and that it is an answer of no consequence ever should you find it. She loves you, still, always, that is the answer."

Gabriel looked at her yet again, and felt that he were really seeing her for the first time. Before him was some kind of being, of a vastly different tenor and nature to his own but bearing all of the unmistakable trappings of sentience, and whether she was in his mind or not mattered not one bit. She sympathised with him, cared and had clearly gone to some lengths to try to alleviate his pain. But most of all she, like himself, like all people, had contemplated death and thought about what it meant, and arrived at conclusions unique to his own. Before him was a person, of this he was irrevocably now convinced. And he trusted her, he believed her. He believed that she had transmitted River's words to him. It was crazy, but crazy in the way that falling in love with River had been. A breathless, benevolent, beckoning crazy that took his hand and didn't have to pull.

River.

Gabriel took a deep breath and was surprised to find how easily his chest inflated, he had laboured so long to draw breath that he had almost completely forgotten that it hadn't always been the case. It was as though a weight had lifted from his every joint and muscle simultaneously, and despite it having been over twenty-four hours since he last slept he felt more awake than ever. Of everything that had happened on this bizarre morning he had predicted this least of all, and the sensation surprised him perhaps even more than first noticing Iris had done. He couldn't begin to rationally conceptualise how any of this had occurred, it seems as though his subconscious mind were calling the shots and only informing him of them after the fact. It was only in it's relief, however temporary it may turn out to be, that he realised just how much he had been hurting before. The release was so palpable that Gabriel felt as though the world around him had exhaled, and the sand beneath him softened.

The Sun had risen now above the horizon, creating a oddly delightful contrast between the yellow warmth of the morning and the warm rain that still saturated the very air he breathed. Across the ocean before him a bold, vibrant Rainbow extended from horizon to horizon, appearing every bit the bridge to a World beyond that myth held it to be. He wasn't sure if it was Iris's presence or simply the density of the rain, but the Rainbow was emblazoned upon the sky behind it with such clarity that he felt sure that he felt sure that he could step and walk upon it, if only it were possible to reach the end. He believed for a moment that he could even succeed, but knew better than to try. There was nothing at it's end that he needed now, nothing that he didn't have here with him. River, loving and his. That was all there was.

A promise. That was what Iris had called it. River had always joked that he was her Guardian Angel, the archangel Gabriel, and he couldn't help but wonder if this might be her mischievous idea of a mythological joke. It would certainly be in accordance with everything he knew of her, and he found himself laughing before he even had a chance to resolve the thought. He briefly considered asking Iris, but quickly dismissed the idea. Somehow this felt private even from her, for the two of them alone. He had always known that it would be she who became an angel for him in the end.

An uncountable plethora of thoughts and feelings settling into place, and Gabriel was accosted by the notion that they had been compelled to all along, waiting only for that suitable disturbance that allows gravity to act. His love for River, the very same love that had for so long been an affliction, had regained it's innocence. He suddenly felt foolish for his behaviour and feelings in the previous months, he had always known their folly of course but seemed to see them clearly for the first time. And yet he didn't feel ashamed of himself, in total contrast to the burning of the photograph in Fiji. He knew that he had always done his best, and coped the best that he could. He just felt that he now had it in him to do a hell of a lot better.

For River.

"The photograph," he said abruptly to himself aloud, that memory having been piqued by this thought, before addressing Iris. "Please tell her I'm so sorry for destroying the photograph, I miss it it so much, I miss her so much, I love her so much...." He trailed off, not sure what else to say. Words seemed so insufficient to express what he was trying to convey, and he gathered from her expression that further attempts weren't necessary.

She looked at him warmly, "Of course, although you don't require me for that. You have done so yourself, perfectly. There is nothing to forgive." She seemed to hesitate for a moment before continuing. "That photograph is not forever lost Gabriel Vance. Two copies existed. River's still survives in the home you left behind. You could bare it for her still."

Gabriel examined her again with new eyes, still not even close to being sure what it was he looked upon. How could she know this, did River provide that information too? Or could he simply have worked it out for himself? It had not occurred to him to search River's inherited possessions for the photograph, he had neither the need nor desire to do so before leaving, but logic dictated that it could still be there. He decided ultimately that it didn't matter. He got the impression that she hadn't been charged (by whatever it was that charged her) to tell him this at all, but that it was a gesture of genuine friendship. She was Iris, goddess and friend, and that was that.

"Why me, why now?" he asked her.

She looked at him curiously, and he got the impression that this was the first question that he had posed her that she had been earnestly not expecting.

"It simply is," she said, "it's what I do."

"I'm sure that's true, but I'm also sure that you didn't have to help me. And that you didn't have to help her. Nobody ever does. You've done more for us than I think even someone like you could ever fully understand. Thank you"

Gabriel wasn't sure where these words came from, he certainly hadn't planned to say them or been conscious of constructing them. But he meant them sincerely, moved by the abrupt intensity of his own compassion.

Iris smiled in a concluding gesture, and Gabriel became aware that her departure was imminent. A wordless bond and understanding flowed freely between them, the kind that would stay with him for the rest of his days. He wondered if it would remain with her too, if it worked that way for whatever she was. He hoped that it did.

"I do have one question though, if I may?" Gabriel said, her stillness signaling her consent. "I was always under the impression that Iris only delivered messages for Hera. Or did the Mythology class get that one wrong?"

Iris looked at him with obvious amusement, "Hera, River, names and distinctions," was all she offered, more as an enigmatic aside than a reply. When he did not respond to this she seemed to catch

117

herself, and said, "I'll have you know that I can deliver messages to and from whomsoever I choose ,thank you very much," flourished with a grin.

He smiled back at her. "Thank you," he said, trying in vain to impress into such simple words the entirety of the emotion that he felt. "I would ask if I'll ever see you again, but I'm sure you would never give me a straight answer."

Iris didn't respond to this other than to continue smiling, and in truth he knew she didn't need to. She was always there, they could both feel it. All that was needed was a bit of sun and water.

"Goodbye, Gabriel Vance," she said with a note of unmistakable finality, and then did something he had not expected: she leaned over fully and kissed him softly upon the cheek before turning to leave. Where her lips touched him, if indeed they could be said to touch, Gabriel could feel a curious sensation, dwelling somewhere between contact and nothingness. Somewhere within it he could unmistakably feel River's distinctive nature, and knew Iris had spoken the truth - she was here within them both. She turned and began to fade away, in the same description-eluding manner with which she performed every action.

"Be careful. I do have a wife, you know."

How Iris responded to this Gabriel would never discover, as she was gone. He was sure she would have laughed.

It was the first joke that Gabriel could recall making in many months. The morning sun was warm and soothing, the gentle breeze rocked the tree under which he lay like a cradle. He hadn't noticed it before, but this place was beautiful, and whilst some party detritus still remained a large portion of the filth on the sand had been dragged away by the rising tide. The rain had stopped now, distracted by the sensational events he was unsure exactly when it had, but it must have been some time ago now as the clouds were already clearing from the sky above.

He was tired and it couldn't hurt to close his eyes for a little while, it would be hours before the hungover residents emerged to trouble him. He had a lot to do, a lot to think about and travel plans back home to make. The road ahead would be long and hard, he would undoubtedly stumble and struggle along it's length, and he knew in his heart that it was at last time to embark upon it. He and hope again for the first time, hope that there just might be something after all of this. But he could worry about all of that when he woke up.

Amphitrite

"The Triumph of Amphitrite" by Hughes Taraval

The Golden Spindle and the Dolphin

by Rebecca Buchanan

"What? No, you don't un — Oh, for crying out — Have you seen the news?!" Naïs waved a handful of socks at the television. She plowed ahead before the booking agent on the other end of the phone could respond. "Oil spill. Massive. Dozens of islands in the Aegean are threatened: fish, dolphins, birds, plants, people. Black sludge all over everything. I need to get there, *now*." She drew a deep breath, tossing the socks onto the bed next to her go bag. "Yes, okay, thank you. I can make that flight. Thank you." She clicked the phone off, dropped it long enough to bundle the socks into a neat roll, and then picked it up again. She hit the first slot on the speed dial, tucked it under her chin, and grabbed another pair. Can never pack too many socks.

It only rang twice.

"Yo, my girl, where you at?" His naturally gravelly voice was half-buried in static, making the words pop and warble.

"Hey, BB. Yeah, I'm coming. Got a flight out of Dublin. I should hit Athens about two o'dark. I'm packing a sample, and shipping the rest straight from the lab. You'll have transport standing by?"

More popping and hissing. "Affirm. Chinook. Gonna be a rough ride. Should be you, a couple salvagers out of Oslo, and a hell of a lot of gear. You gonna be ready to work when you get here?"

Naïs grinned. "Affirm. When am I not ready to work?"

BB's chuckle was a snarl of whistles and pops. "You need to slow down, girl. Come up for air. Enjoy the swim."

"Sure. When idiots stop dumping toxic sludge in the ocean, on purpose or 'accidentally.' Then I'll slow down. See you in a few."

She hung up, zipped the bag, threw it over her shoulder, and was out the door. She forgot to turn off the television.

II

Her flight was late, held up in Paris when a connecting flight out of New York ran into a late spring snowstorm. It was well after three in the morning before she cleared customs ("No! Not poison! Not bomb! Powdered beeswax! UNEERT, you know, United Nations? I need that!") and almost four when her harried cab driver pulled up next to the helipad. She hauled her go bag off the seat beside her, tossed him a handful of euros, and dashed towards the open rear hatch of the squat Chinook.

She flashed her id at a guy with a bright yellow vest and a clipboard. He nodded, shoved a visored helmet into her hands, and waved her aboard. He turned away, speaking in rapid Greek into the radio strapped to his shoulder.

The belly of the fat, gray chopper was already stuffed with equipment and containers; some she recognized, but not all. The stacked boxes, held in place by a thick netting, were covered in a dozen different languages: French, Spanish, Portuguese, Turkish, Hebrew, Arabic, Russian, and —

"*Hallo!*"

— Norwegian.

Broad shoulders, brilliant blue eyes, an easy grin, and the beginnings of a beard. Thick blond curls poked out from beneath his helmet. He waved as she shoved her bag beneath the seat across from him and dropped tiredly into place.

"*Hallo,*" she returned, fighting a yawn.

"Kjartan Bue, Oslo, salvage." He held out his hand.

She snapped her harness, tightened the lap belt, and returned his handshake. "Naïs Wright, Dublin, marine ecologist." She slipped on the helmet, grimacing at the tight fit.

The rear hatch groaned and squeaked, closing with a loud *grunch*. The overhead lights flickered.

He grinned wider, his voice echoing oddly over the radio. "Eh? You don't sound very Irish."

She leaned her head back, trying to find a comfortable place for her shoulders. The Chinook vibrated as the double rotors started to spin. "Dublin by way of Pensacola."

"Ah." He nodded, voice rising as the sound of the rotors penetrated the hull. "You the Naïs Wright who worked on the *Konstantin* and the *Jamileh*? The lady with the beeswax?"

She closed her eyes. "Yep. And the lady with the beeswax needs a nap."

"Ah, *ja*, of course. My apologies." He was almost yelling now. "We talk later."

"Sure," she muttered as she drifted off, the chopper bouncing as it laboriously lifted away from the ground and swung towards the heart of the Aegean.

III

The wreck lay ten kilometers off the northwestern coast of Limnos. Tiny boats armed with powerful lights huddled around it, casting weird shadows; the beginnings of a floating tactical platform was a slash of white and red in the shadow of the ruined ship. A huge tear bisected the front port hull where the *Anastasiya* had collided with the smaller *Meryem*. The latter now sat on the bottom of the Aegean, along with two of her crew. The *Anastasiya*, gushing oil and listing badly, would soon join her unless the salvagers could repair the worst of the damage and get the tanker stabilized. Shimmering, the oil spread out from the wreck, surrounded by kilometer after kilometer of snaking, bright orange booms.

Kjartan unhooked his harness and leaned around her to peer out the tiny window. He whistled. "That there's gonna be a bit of work."

Naïs scowled as the Chinook swooped around the wreck, heading towards the *Mater Salacia*. The UNEERT's carrier floated another kilometer beyond the *Anastasiya*, her deck a swarm of activity. Naïs' fingers twitched, her chest tight with anticipation and anxiety.

"You got enough beeswax to clean up all that?" Kjartan asked.

Her lips tightened. "No," she conceded. "It's still experimental. I only have half a liter with me. I'm having ten liters shipped in, should be here in a few hours." She twisted further in her seat, trying to keep the spill in view as the chopper banked and prepared to land. "Please tell me they haven't started spraying the dispersant yet."

"Ehhh … *Nei*, doesn't appear so. Just deployed the booms, so far." He grinned at her again, teeth flashing, as he dropped into his seat and clicked his harness. "Looks like you'll get the chance to try your stuff. Let's hear it for the bees, eh?"

The Chinook thunked onto the deck with a tooth-jarring thud, metal and rubber creaking, rotors gradually slowing. Crew in bright yellow and green and red vests dodged around one another, dragging hoses, hefting cargo, waving clipboards, yelling into their headsets and at one another. The rear hatch groaned and fell open, revealing a battered, frumpy BB.

"You're late," he growled. Scraggly, mismatched patches of beard covered the lower half of his face and poked out of the collar of his shirt. Sweat trickled down his face from beneath his helmet.

Naïs shoved off her harness. "Not my fault at — "

"Not you." He jerked a thumb over his shoulder. "Rest of your team is already out at the site, Kjartan. Get your gear and take the next boat out to the tactical platform."

The Norwegian saluted smartly, still grinning, and started hauling crates out of the helicopter.

"Okay, now it's your turn." BB opened his arms wide and pulled her into a bone-crushing hug. She grunted, one arm pinned between them, the other clutching the strap of her bag. "How you been, girl?"

"Busy," she huffed, trying to draw breath.

He let go and held her back at arms' length, inspecting her up and down. "You got circles under your eyes, you aren't eating enough — again — and how long's it been since you been laid?"

"Oh, whatever." Naïs shoved his hands away.

BB waved her to follow him and set off across the deck. Crew danced and dodged around them. "You need a vacation, girl. Just relax and be in the moment."

"How about you take your own advice?"

"I did. Bora Bora." They ducked instinctively as the Chinook lifted away, wind tearing at their clothes, the vibrations from the rotors shaking their bones. BB continued, "Had to after the *Jamileh*. A whole month of mai tais, snorkeling, and topless bikinis. You should try it. Do your soul some good." He twisted the handle on the metal door and shoved it open, ushering her inside. The noise level dropped noticeably when it closed behind them.

BB pulled off his helmet and ran a dirty cloth over his bare, shaved scalp. Naïs followed suit, grimacing; not much to be done with helmet-flattened hair.

"I'll think about it," she finally responded. "I don't suppose my package is here yet?"

"Yep." Her head whipped up in surprise at his answer. "Came in on the chopper right before you. Guess it wasn't held up, like you were."

"Wher — "

"Ah." He held up a hand. "Demonstration first. Some bigwigs are here. They want to see you and your beeswax in action." He took her helmet and handed both off to a young crewwoman with yet another clipboard. He waggled a finger. "Thisaway."

"What, now?" she squeaked.

"You're the one who said you'd be ready to work."

She stumbled after him down the corridor, bag suddenly heavy in her hands. "Just how big are these wigs?"

"The Greek Minister of Environment, Energy, and Climate Change; the Turkish Minister of Environment and Urban Planning; the Director of the European Environment Agency; and — " his eyebrows danced " — Director-General Karine-Liliane Benjelloun of the United Nations Environmental Emergency Response Team."

IV

Naïs cleared her throat once, and then again. "Good morning, ladies and gentlemen, Ministers, Director-General." Lots of people. Lots of people in suits wearing serious expressions. Not just the Ministers and the Director-General, but all of their aides and assistants and translators and who knew who else, all crowded around a ceramic and metal table in the belly of the *Mater Salacia*. A tub of seawater, lined with oily sludge, sat in the center of the table. It reeked. A few of the suits were not so subtly covering their noses behind their hands, taking shallow breaths. BB stood somewhere way at the back of the crowd; she caught the occasional flash of his bare head in the lights.

Naïs cleared her throat for a third time. *Make the spiel*, she thought. *It'll work.* "Oil spills on land and especially at sea are an unfortunate and all too common event in our modern industrial age. The Gulf War, the *Deepwater Horizon*, the *Konstantin* and the *Jamileh*, to name just a few examples. There are many ways to deal with these spills. Unfortunately, some are just as damaging to the environment as the oil itself — some even more so. In recent years, corporations, nonprofit organizations, governmental agencies, and international organizations — " she nodded at the Director-General " — have been working to develop less-destructive, more environmentally-friendly alternatives. Such as ...." She held up the half-liter vial. The golden powder shifted inside, shimmering. "Saltwater petroleum bioremediation for deep level exposure. Or, to make a useable acronym out of that, SPinDLE."

The Director-General quirked a dark eyebrow at her.

The Turkish Minister leaned forward, thick mustache twitching. "Was this not used before? The *Jamileh* wreck, yes?"

"Yes, i — "

"And it was a failure."

Naïs tightened her jaw. "SPinDLE was still in very early testing stages when it was deployed at the *Jamileh*. Before then, it had only been used in the lab, under controlled conditions. We knew going in that SPinDLE would not take care of the spill, that more conventional means would have to be used — but we had to test it in the field, to gather the necessary data to make adjustments to its compos — "

The Greek Minister broke in. "And how much time and money have been spent conducting these tests and making these adjustments?"

" ... I don't have exact figures, but the results have been promising."

The Turkish Minister snorted.

Naïs charged ahead. "Petroleum bioremediation capsules were originally discovered by NASA — accidentally, I might add. Composed of thousands of hollow beeswax spheres, 0.25- to 0.65-μm in diameter, with hollow centers, the microspheres are impervious to water, but the oil is sucked right in. The beeswax also attracts naturally-occurring oceanic microbes which break down the oil. Add some Pseudomonas bacteria to the mix, which loves to dine on the hydrocarbons in the petroleum, breaking it down into water and carbon dioxide, and you have the perfect, nontoxic oil eater."

The Turkish Minister's mustache twitched again. "Then why did you fail with the *Jamileh*?"

Naïs felt her teeth grinding.

Director-General Benjelloun waved an elegant brown hand at the tub. "Dr. Wright, if you would, please."

"Yes, ma'am." Holding her breath, Naïs pulled the stopper off the vial and tipped it, spreading the modified beeswax across the surface of the water. It glowed warmly in the ship's light for a moment, then slowly began to sink.

Naïs exhaled, almost whispering. "To the naked eye, SPinDLE looks like a blanket. Under a microscope, though, it is a fine, golden net."

The beeswax rippled softly as it settled on top of the thick sludge. The Ministers and their aides and assistants and translators and who knew who else leaned forward, pushing against one another, craning their necks.

"Beeswax is naturally lighter than saltwater, so it floats. That makes it ideal for *surface* spills. Go lower than about three or four meters, and you're out of luck. SPinDLE took care of the oil on the surface around the *Jamileh* — in record time and with no ill effects. Clean-up crews even said it smelled nice." She saw BB smother a laugh. "But not the sludge that sank a hundred meters down to the bottom of the strait. We needed to figure out how to make SPinDLE heavier, without adding toxic elements, such as heavy metals or synthetics … and we've succeeded." *I hope.*

As they watched, the sludge gradually disappeared, receding down the edges of the tub and across the bottom. The golden blanket swelled. And then, one by one, the microspheres began to burst.

"The microorganism population expands almost exponentially, feeding on the wax and the oil, breaking them down. As their food supply dwindles, the microorganism population returns to normal … and the environment is restored."

The last of the sludge evaporated in a swirl of bubbles.

Silence.

The Director-General rested her hands on the table, staring at the clean tub of saltwater. When she finally looked up, a soft smile curled the edge of her mouth. "When can you start?"

V

"*Hallo* again, beeswax lady!"

"Hello, again, *Herr* Bue." Naïs scrubbed a hand across her face, squinting in the bright afternoon sunlight. She could taste petroleum on her tongue. She shifted her rebreather on her left shoulder, clambering over the side of the boat and onto the tactical platform. Director-General Benjelloun had needed to talk to her, then this Minister, then that Minister, then BB and the skipper and the director of salvage operations and there was the diving schedule to go over and topographical maps and current charts and on and on .... How many hours had she slept? Three? Four?

He waved his hand, grinning. The wind pulled at his curls, offering a brief respite from the stink of the spill. "*Nei, nei.* Call me Kjartan. We are diving together, yes? We should use Christian names."

She made her way towards the large cylinder on the far side of the platform, a pair of deflated yellow pontoons strapped to either side of

133

it. The deck was a blazing white and red beneath her feet. Her eyes began to hurt. She looked away, focusing on the *Anastasiya*; the wreck loomed over them, only a hundred meters away. She could make out some of the salvage crew on the tilted deck and hanging in harnesses down the side. At least the tear had punctured only two of the interior tanks, and not all five.

She shook her head, looking away. "Mom was a well-read hippie. She named me after an Amazon queen in some old poem. Definitely not a Christian name."

He skipped after her. "A heathen after my own heart, then. I think I should like your mother."

Naïs snorted a laugh. "Well, next time you're in Pensacola, be sure to look her up. She lives in the converted tugboat with the greenhouse on the front deck. She's ... well-known."

"Ah, I think you mean a different word, but are too polite to say it."

"You're probably right." She stopped next to the ladder; miniature booms set around it created a half-circle of clear blue sea water. "You set?"

"*Ja.*" He thumped the large cylinder. "SPinDLE is ready to go. Got a couple of DPVs to get us down faster. Liev and Sivert — " he waved at the two broad-shouldered, blonde men idling in a small boat a few meters away, its sides slick and black " — will be monitoring from up here, following our path. They'll catch the pod when it comes back up."

She swung her rebreather onto her back and settled the mask over her eyes and nose. "Then let's not waste anymore time."

VI

It was dark beneath the spill, a dim twilight, not the pure crystalline blue-green for which the Aegean was known. Their shadows bounced and twisted oddly through the water, only to be swallowed by the sludge that covered the sea floor. Crude oil dribbled down around them in thick ribbons and globs. Naïs could pick out the shapes of rocks and ridges and corals. Anemones and sea grasses contorted this way and that, weighted down, their colors muted. Fish swam in confused circles, eyes big. In the distance, a pod of dolphins dipped to the bottom, poked at the sludge, then hastily lifted away, only to return again, chattering urgently.

The oil spread out in a rough fan shape from beneath the *Anastasiya*, the lower, faster currents carrying it a good two kilometers out from the wreck.

Not enough beeswax. Not nearly enough.

She tightened her grip on the handle of the DPV, the thrum of its rotor making her skin prickle. She cast a quick glance over at Kjartan. He nodded down, lifting a hand from his own DPV long enough to point towards one particular sludge-coated ridge. She returned the nod and they angled down, the double nylon rope which ran from their

DPVs back to the SPinDLE momentarily pulling taut.

Darker.

The *Anastasiya* was a wounded, bleeding colossus, a creaking shadow in the stained water. They switched on their headlamps and the twin lamps on the DPVs.

Naïs cut the engine on her DPV, Kjartan following suit. Momentum carried them forward another few meters, the nylon rope going slack as the cylinder slid up between them. Naïs grabbed one of the deflated pontoons, holding it still. She forced her fingers to loosen, running her hand across the pod's smooth surface. Anxiety and anger twisted her stomach.

A touch.

She started, looking over to find Kjartan's gloved hand resting atop her own. He tilted his head, bubbles fizzing from his rebreather. She inhaled once and then again, trying to settle her stomach.

Nope. Still angry.

Pulling her hand away, she pointed towards the near end of the ridge line. He hesitated a moment, then gave her a thumb's up. They powered up their DPVs again, gliding steadily down, down, down, SPinDLE secure between them.

Darker.

Their headlamps were spears of golden-white light. Fish darted through the light, disoriented, and turtles blinked, shells dirty. They found the ridge line and spun around so that they were facing towards the *Anastasiya* and its roiling wound. Naïs slid her hand along the top of the cylinder and down the back side until she found the release valve. A quick twist and a flick and part of the back panel flipped open. A moment of nothing when she stopped breathing, and then a swirl of gold.

The beeswax floated out and then down, a warm, lacy blanket. It shimmered and rippled, knitting together, beginning to swell even as it dropped through the water towards the seabed. Naïs watched, lips too tight around her mouthpiece, her stomach a knot. She reminded herself to breathe. She let the DPV pull her forward, head craned around so that she could watch SPinDLE deploy. It spread across the ridge behind them, outlining every crevice and point and dip, every coral and anemone and blade of seagrass. The golden blanket expanded, here and there a microcapsule exploding in a burst of oxygen and hydrogen.

Farther they went, the rotors of the DPVs humming, their headlamps swinging back and forth. Closer to the *Anastasiya*, a fine golden netting spreading out in their wake.

A dolphin skimmed passed, chittering, head bobbing. Kjartan stretched out a hand, just managing to brush the mammal's glistening side before it suddenly kicked away.

A rumble in the water, a grinding and shrieking of metal. Kjartan jerked on the cylinder, pulling her roughly to the side. She looked around as the ocean surged around her, fish fleeing in panic. The horrible sound vibrated through her bones.

A shift in the darkness, a break in the gloom.

Naïs looked up as the oil on the surface momentarily parted, allowing a few seconds of sunlight to break through — long enough for her to see the section of the *Anastasiya*'s hull break away and plunge through the sea, falling, falling, falling, falling, blocking her view of the sky, of the sea, of Kjartan —

VII

Dark.

A touch. Warm liquid sliding across her cheek.

A voice, not in her ears, but along her skin, in her head. *It is hers?*

Yes. A different voice. *What is it?*

Of the bees, the gift of Hermes. A third voice.

The second voice again. *My Queen! Divine One, look! It takes the poison!*

Silence. Another soft touch at her forehead. Vaguely, she wondered where her mask could have gone. Did she drop it?

The first voice, firm, but kind. *Waken, little one.*

Naïs peeled her eyes open. Colors swirled, blues and greens and blacks and stark whites. The water was … solid. There was a form there, in the water, of the water. She blinked. Three shapes. Female, yes, definitely female: long hair that trailed away into the current, round breasts, supple waists that flowed down into shimmering tails. The colors bled together, then apart, whirled around within the watery form.

Somewhere in the back of her brain, she knew she should be panicking — but her heart was steady, her breathing even. Breathing water. She felt … warm, safe.

You brought us this gift, little one? The closest figure, the first speaker, lifted a hand, microcapsules glimmering.

Yes, I —

Did you also bring the poison which suffocates my children, which taints my waters and hides the holy sun? The voice hardened, and she felt some of the warmth drift away, cold settling into her bones.

No! No! That was an accident! The poison is not mine —

Then whose is it, if not yours?

One of the figures, the third one, slipped around Naïs, tangling water fingers in her hair, pulling at her head.

It's not — ow! It is ours! It is all of ours! The fingers loosened a bit. *The poison is for our machines. It is … it is how we travel and work and … we know the poison is bad. We're trying to fix it, we are, to do better. BB and Kjartan and Benjelloun*

139

and — and — so many. We're trying to fix it ... it was an accident ... we're trying to do better ....

The watery fingers left her hair, the third figure sliding into view again.

The first speaker seemed to consider her for a moment. A dolphin (the same from before?) slipped by, rubbing up against the closest water woman. His silvery hide reflected the whirl of colors. She ran a hand along its back and the dolphin blew bubbles in delight.

You are angry, little one. I can taste the anger in your blood, and the shame.

... Yes.

The water woman twirled her finger, spinning the golden beeswax into a corkscrew. It thickened, tightened, and, for a brief moment, it took on the shape of one of the spindles of old. Then the beeswax dispersed, dropped, weaving back into a net as it settled onto the ocean floor.

A gift of the bees, yes; but not of you. It is recompense, rightly offered — and accepted. The woman, the mermaid, the Queen, swirled closer, greens and blues and blacks and whites brilliant. She wound around Naïs, grasp firm but not threatening. *This is recompense you shall continue to make, until you have learned from the error of your ways and ceased to make use of this poison — or until Mother Gaia grows tired of your insolence and lets loose her furious daughters.* A hand tangled in Naïs' hair again, pulling back her head, while a

140

second hand slid down her chest and settled over her heart. *A reminder.*

And then she was free, floating, the colorful beings swimming away, disappearing into the distance. Darkness settled around her, warmth bleeding away. Salty water filled her nose and mouth. She flailed, trying not to breathe, kicking, flapping, dark, she couldn't see ....

Hands. Hands pulling hard. Something rubbery was shoved into her mouth. Air. She could breathe. She inhaled again and again, feeling her body being pulled along. Light. Not so dark now ....

They broke the surface. Coughing, she spat out the mouthpiece. She tried to kick, but her legs were too heavy. She squinted, the sun burning her eyes. More hands, pulling her up and over. Blonde, broad shoulders. Right, the boat. The Norwegians. What were their names again?

"Liev and Sivert," she coughed. "Nice to meet you." She vomited more water. Kjartan held her up, supporting her while she leaned over the side of the boat. Her chest felt funny, right over her heart. When she was finally done, able to breathe normally again, he lowered her into one of the seats.

He pushed the hair off her forehead, eyes narrowed in concern. "Okay there, beeswax lady?"

She nodded. "My hero. How long?"

"'Bout two minutes, maybe a bit more."

Two minutes. She shivered. Long enough for cold and shock and oxygen deprivation to play havoc with her brain .... Right. That made sense.

141

Kjartan's jaw tightened. "Thought I was gonna be bringing your body back to the *Salacia*. BB woulda killed me."

Naïs started to laugh, which turned into another coughing fit. The pressure on her chest eased, turned warm. She rubbed at the spot with the heel of her hand. "SPinDLE?"

"Other than part of the ship falling on top of us?" He gestured out at the water. "See for yourself."

The cylinder floated nearby, the inflated yellow pontoons hugging it; a huge dent marred one side. The water around it bubbled and fizzled, the surface oil dancing as the microcapsules exploded, the sludge far below dispersing. The wind carried the sounds of cheering from the nearby tactical platform, and the radio crackled with excited whoops.

VIII

The Director-General met them at the hatch, shaking Naïs' hand, congratulating her. Then one Minister, then another Minister, and another, and all their aides and assistants and translators and who knew who else; and BB, who crushed her into a tight hug and whispered something about Bora Bora; and finally the chief medical officer, who shoved Naïs and Kjartan onto matching gurneys and hauled them away.

Naïs was poked and prodded and bandaged. She hadn't even realized that there was a cut on her left arm and a gash in her forehead. Neither hurt. There was only the weird, tingly pressure in her chest. Finally, the nurses dumped them into matching bunks with machines to monitor their heart rate and breathing. The CMO insisted on jabbing an IV into Naïs' arm. And, then, finally, the doctor was gone, too, and there was only the beeping of the machines and the distant rumble of the engine and the thrum of helicopters.

"So, what's your well-read hippie mother think of that tattoo?" Kjartan asked.

Naïs blinked, rolling her head towards him. "Sorry?"

"The tattoo, beeswax lady." He grinned. "Maybe I need to change your nickname, *ja*?"

Naïs pressed a fist to that tight, warm spot between her ribs. "I … uh …. I don't …. 'Scuse me a second."

She shoved the blanket aside and squirmed to the edge of the bed. Her legs shook as she dropped her feet to the floor, her toes curling against the cold metal. Biting her lips, she pushed herself upright, lifted the IV bag free of its hook, and made her way over to the bathroom.

She flicked on the light, swallowing as she caught sight of her reflection in the mirror. The hospital gown was too big, making her look skinny and underfed. Her skin was too pale, blood vessels standing out blue. A bright white bandage wound around her head, another around her left forearm. She pushed the door closed.

Drawing a deep breath, feeling the warm, smooth pressure, she tugged down the collar of the gown. Lower and lower. The first tie hit the back of her neck, snagged, then pulled loose. The top of the gown dropped below her breasts.

It was there, just slightly left of center. A dolphin, done in the ancient Minoan style: bright blue on the top, a squiggly horizontal line down its middle, a white bottom. The dolphin was curled into a tight circle, surrounding her heart.

For just a moment, the dolphin seemed to flex and she felt fingers lightly trace across her cheek. And then it was still again, and there was only the sound of her own heartbeat and the rush of her saltwater blood.

[Author's Note: petroleum remediation product is real. It was discovered and developed by NASA in the early 1990s. Universal Remediation Inc. commercialized the product, and now offers it in a variety of forms to both individuals and corporations. It is one of the most safe and effective means for cleaning up oil spills large or small. To my knowledge, no one has yet figured out how to make it sink.]

Amphitrite

by Emily May

(she said)
i have risen from the water
to give you this, love;

take these fish from my palms,
the whalebone from my throat. their
silvery pulses will stay with you
forever (as if I had returned,
I was home! she said)

take my song, my gull-cries,
my shuddering lungs in the dark

for you are i, and we are one,
belonging to the same shoal, so afraid
of our own soul and mind, swimming
sad and incomplete
(she swum in
my head, churned in my gulping throat, she cried)

abide in my breast and my fifty kisses
(and with that she was gone, a gem of salt
in my eye)

Hymn to Amphitrite I

by Rebecca Buchanan

salt-tongued
queen of the sea
at the heart of the world:
nude
but for the net
draped round your hips
and the single strand of pearls
smoky grey
round one slim ankle:
your laughter
the sun upon the waves

Amphitrite, The Third One Who Encircles

by Shoshana Sarah

I watched the copper moon
heavy and saturated sag in
the night of its weighted
descent beneath umbels of constellations
I listened to the infinite heave-ho symphony of
the tides (really just a cacophony of things I can't
       hear)
incessantly crashing from the eternal night
to the edge of my feet
I walked in — wimples discarded to the shores —
uninhibited as Ishtar[1]
but I am Amphitrite[2] as I glide into the folds
of the Mediterranean with my hands free
~I am the tide-breaker~
I challenged the universe in the time
of Aquarius on the waves
I saw myself walk on the water
deeper and further into deafening darkness
to find him and save her

We were three actually
~I am the third one who encircles~
three souls sui generis
we share a telepathy
beyond all physical intimacies
Three oracles
Three sirens

Three mythological siblings
Three threads spun in the tapestry of
consciousness from the same flax
Three points of light which met at the
center of the world (in seriatim)
and formed a beacon in the eye of
the maelstrom
An ecumenical holy trinity:
the Mason
the Healer
and the Jewess
He and I tell her:
tu fui ego eris
I was what you are; what I am, you will be

Notes:

1) Ishtar is the ancient Sumero-Babylonian goddess of love, fertility, sexuality, healing and war. She is cognate with the Greek Goddess Aphrodite, the Assyrian Goddess Astarte, and the Sumerian goddess Inanna. In the Babylonian pantheon she "was the divine personification of the planet Venus." Her cult involved sacred prostitution as the goddess of courtesans.

2) In Greek mythology, Amphitrite is a sea-goddess (of the Mediterranean) and wife of Poseidon. Her Roman counterpart is Salacia. Her name is interpreted as "the third one who encircles [the sea]", "the surrounding third," or "the third one who encircles (everything)" (because the ancient Greeks thought the whole world was encircled by a river-god, Oceanus). Her name is also said to mean the "third element," which is the sea.

"Poseidon" by KS Roy

Written on the Waves

by Jennifer Lawrence

I have never seen the ocean, save
As pictures in books, on TV, in film,
And yet I feel your tidal rhythms
Flow through me,
Too powerful to be denied.
Fearful in the way that all deep
And unexplored reaches are fearful —
Abrim with strange treasure:
Coral reef, pearl bank, little fish like gems
Spangling those dark and liquid depths
— and you, serene and stormy by turns,
Undisputed monarch
White-bearded with whitecap foam
And I, so small in comparison,
Chained by unseen bonds,
(Your salt tides
Ebb and rip in my blood)
Can only bow in silent awe.

To Poseidon Hippios

by Terence Ward

Hail Hippios, thundering lord of horses!
There is no distinction between
the pounding of the surf,
the rumble of the rocks,
the surging of my heart, and
the thunder of the hooves.
Human labor would never be
human mastery without these beasts.
But human failings can ever forget
the debts we owe, greatest to least.
Hippios, with your horses as partners
our people have thrived,
sharing our labors and
permitting our rides.
May our people remember
this gift that you gave
and honor your horses
as companions, not slaves.

Lord of Aegae

by Juleigh Howard-Hobson

I rule wet depths, known or unknown. I rule
Murk and bone, fin and sinew, down below.
I rule cresting wave, crashing breakers, cool
Flashes of tumbling blue walls that come, go,
Come, go again and again with no end
To their action at my edges, yet still
I rule them; every shore is me, I blend
Sand and sea, beach and foam. I reach until
There is no more to claim. All of the brine,
All of the creatures, all of the churning
Ebbing coursing things of water are mine.
I rule the leaving and the returning
Waves. I rule the undertows and the tides
That wait for my command before they rise.

Poseidon Night

by Sandy Hiortdahl

I dream of you, Sea God, climbing over the edge
of my make-shift raft and making love to me
as we sail West into Apollo's sunset, heading for
the Artemis moon, while Gemini rises over the
          waves,
and dolphins mark our passage with their song.
You smile at a seahawk's call to us and we
drift into Triton Bay, warm together,
your eyes above me, and we do not heed the gulls,
nor the gentle bump of sea turtles coming closer to
          greet you.

To Poseidon,
Lord of the Seas and More

by Ann Hatzakis

XXII. To Poseidon

I begin to sing about Poseidon, the great god, mover
      of the earth and barren sea,
the sea-god who is lord of Helikon and broad
      Aigai.
O Earth-shaker, two-fold is your god-given
      prerogative,
to be a tamer of horses and a savior of ships.
Hail, Poseidon, black-maned holder of the earth!
Have a kindly heart, O blessed one, and come to the
      aid of sailors!

17. To Poseidon

(incense -- myrrh)

Hearken, dark-maned Poseidon, holder of the earth.
horse god, you hold the bronze trident in your hand,
you dwell in the foundations of the full-bosomed
sea.

Shaker of the earth, deep-roaring ruler of the
waters, the waves are your blossoms, O gracious
one, as you urge horses and chariots on rushing on
the sea, splashing through the rippling brine.

The unfathomable sea fell to your lot, the third
portion. Waves and their wild dwellers please you,

156

O spirit of the deep. May you save the foundations of the earth and ships moving at full tilt, bringing peace, health, and blameless prosperity.

Although most people only see the god Poseidon as the Lord of the Seas, both these hymns hint at there being a broader view of Him in ancient Greece. He is the Lord of horses and Earth-shaker — both of these things dealing more with land than sea. The *Homeric Hymn* even states that his prerogative is not just in dealing with the oceans. Not only that, both of the hymns indicate that he has a responsibility for the foundations of the earth as he is "holder of the earth" in the *Homeric Hymn* and the *Orphic Hymn* asks him to "save the foundations of the earth". These things are ones that as a Hellenic Polytheist who lives inland, are ways that I can still connect with him and honor him as we go into the winter season in the Northern Hemisphere — when the Athenian calendar assigns him a month (sometimes two) in his honor.

There are many people who do not hold this god as being important inland — because he is just the "sea-god" in their eyes, but as the health of the oceans impacts the land, this is not a view I can support. We as polytheists and servants of the Gods have a duty to protect the gifts we are given by them. We cannot ignore the responsibility we have been given by putting it on others if we are to teach our children to honor the things that the Gods represent and rule over.

The ways that I can honor Poseidon inland are not necessarily different than the ways I honored Him when I lived nearer to the coast, but that is because we can perform libations and other offerings anywhere — even in our kitchens. A figurine of a rearing horse can serve as well as a statue of Poseidon sitting on a seashell encrusted throne holding his trident. On my home shrine of the Olympians, Poseidon is not even represented by something even that obvious — what represents Him is a small jar with sand, water and plastic fish in it that my pre-schooler made while studying the sea and sea life and, as it is hand-made, can serve just as well as any more elaborate and "traditional-looking statue of the God."

We are restoring a vibrant faith to life, and one of the ways we can do this is by helping our children to learn about the Gods, not only teaching them the ancient myths, but also showing them everyday household rituals in honor of the Gods. We also need to create ways to honor the Gods that help our children connect to the Gods wherever we are — inland or sea-side. To honor the God of the rolling waves, who is also the Lord and Father of horses, we can take a boat ride **or** a trail ride. We can give to charities that support wild mustangs or campaign for an end to whaling. What we cannot do is be complacent in our faith. That is something that we must never do — especially when it comes to the realms of the Sons of Cronos.

Poseidon was perhaps the most important of the sons of Cronos in the everyday lives of the ancient Greeks even though his brother Zeus was the King of the Gods and his brother Hades the Lord of the Underworld. It is because they were intimately connected to His moods in their everyday lives and because of this assigned a month in their calendar named in His honor (a month that coincidentally corresponds to the time of year when sailing is the most dangerous in the Mediterranean). We cannot always go to the sea if we live over a day's travel inland, as many of us now do, but we can still honor him in the waters of the earth, over which he also has dominion, as well as in the earth herself as we find the incidence of earthquakes increasing in parts of the world. We can petition that he preserve the sailor and land-liver alike. And we can remember that modern science tells us that all animal life originated in Poseidon's domain and because of that we carry the seas within our bodies and spirits wherever we are in the world.

It is for this reason that we still pour libations to Him and celebrate the Poseidea festival. This festival is not well documented, unfortunately, so I can't provide a lot of details on it. Some ways to celebrate it in the modern era include visiting the seashore if possible, or surrounding ourselves with symbolism of the Sea and things connected with it. Reciting, as well as meditating on, the *Homeric* and

Orphic Hymns in honor of Poseidon is part of this celebration in the modern era as well. Remember when doing this to honor both His role as Lord of the Wine-dark sea as well as his roles as Horse-lord and Earth-shaker. On a personal note, I would also recommend remembering his role as a purifier due to the fact that sea-salt baths for purification are something that the ancients used and that we also use in the modern day. Ask him to help cleanse us of the miasma of everyday living that often accumulates in our lives during the early part of the winter season (in the Northern Hemisphere) and ask his help in keeping us in a state where we are prepared to honor the rest of the Theoi.

To Poseidon Hudsonios

by Terence Ward

Of all the places Poseidon touches
by current, by surf, by rhythm of tide,
none so clearly he holds as the river called Hudson
from its mountainous sources to its bay, deep and
       wide.

Named Hudson by English, North by the Dutch,
and "drowned" by scholars eschewing gestalt,
Poseidon is wed to this river's great spirit
as known by the far-flung presence of salt.

No other river so thoroughly knows
the touch of the ocean upon its twin shores.
With a flick of his trident in the deep of the sea
Poseidon bids, "Retreat now from me."

River and ocean, one and the same
unlike other unions that are beheld.
No subsuming this spirit, absorbing its name —
rather a union, as gods choose to meld.

Offering

by Jennifer Lawrence

I had lived all my life within a stone's throw of
water, yet never before had I seen the ocean.
(With my own eyes, that is, in person:
television and movies didn't count, nor photos,
lovely as they might be; experience is everything.)

We arrived just before lunch that day, the heat of the
    sun
beating down above us, bringing beads of our own
    saltwater
up from the wells of our pores: foresight in the
    flesh.

I had swum in the Mississippi, in Lake Michigan, in
various smaller streams and ponds: they were not
    You.
Born under the sign of Cancer, how I longed to
    meet You:
what water-baby would not?

I had planned, prepared to greet You, pleased at the
    chance,
knowing it might never happen again. Biloxi is not
    Atlantis,
but it sits on the Atlantic, and that is Your domain,
    too.

The Gulf of Mexico is far from the Aegean, but still
            it was
inevitable that no single atom of water there had
            never
once crashed in waves against the shore near
            Athens:
flowing, fluid, flickering under sunlight, flashing
            waves bright.

I brought wine, the best I could manage; a white
            wine,
not the reds I always offered Apollo and Athena and
            Dionysus and Hermes.
White like water is, as it trickles through my
            fingers,
and the fish on the label seemed apt enough.

When I got out of the car, I was barefoot, and the
            white sand
was hot under my soles. Hermit crabs crisscrossed
            the beach in
slow parade, leaving their crooked trails behind
            them; if my shadow
splashed across their shells, they went still, waiting
            for the threat to pass.

And at last, I stepped into your waters.

Warm, they were — so warm, it felt like an
            embrace.
How long had I waited for this?

Perhaps since I swam in that other ocean, amniotic
        bliss enfolding me;
I became conscious of the salt spray
catching my cheeks as each wave hit the shore,
or perhaps that saltwater came from somewhere
        else,
joyful tears at meeting You for the first time.

I waded out to my knees, daring but not too daring;
I had seen jellyfish dying on the beach,
had no wish to meet them and join them. Your realm
        is not
without its risks, as every fisher and sailor and
        swimmer knows.

I had opened the wine bottle before stepping from
        sand into surf,
and now listened, just listened:
        hearing the gulls scream as they wheeled
overhead,
        hearing the crash of every wave behind me
as it hit the sand,
        hearing the far-off echo of boat horns,
        and hearing, at last, Your voice.

"O father Poseidon, I come to You here,
meeting You in Your realm,
the ocean where all life began.
I bring a gift — meager, but well-meant —
to express my joy, my gratitude, my love.
I ask nothing in return: the bliss I know now

164

as I stand in Your waters is gift enough."

And I poured out my libation out to You.

Father Poseidon, forgive me if some nights
I dream of that ocean, of those warm and
         welcoming waters,
the cries of gulls and the crashing sounds of waves,
that music that will haunt me to the end of my days,
and pray that some day, perhaps You will grant me a
         gift,
and I might somehow find a way to return,
and pay homage to you once more.

<u>Hymn to Poseidon</u>

by Mari

Dark-bearded sovereign of the waves,
Poseidon Pelegaios abides in the deep water.
Lances of sunlight scatter into gold
that gleams in his horses' manes
and along the friezes of his palace.
In the wake of his chariot, the waters still;
sinuous monsters frolic alongside,
aphotic pale and ghastly.

The tempestuous lord, sea-green
and furious with the sea's rage
when his pride is crossed,
roars with the thunder of hooves;
Ennosigaios strikes the earth.
Beneath the butt of his trident,
the ground convulses; the tormented
surf churns. At his command,
the waters rise, the cliffs shudder;
at his command, they subside again.

Mighty god who raises colossal walls,
overshadows coastal cities and wraps
them in his protection, and bridles
wild-charging horses, Asphalios
cherishes harbors and wraps them
in imported linens and finespun wools.
He drapes his cities in the treasures
of trading ships and the ocean depths.

Fearsome warrior, father of heroes,
mounted on dolphins and seahorses,
the god of the oceans surges like the tides,
ferocious and merry and bright and fierce.
None holds my heart, compels my every love,
like the silver, turquoise, dark son of Kronos,
lord of all the waters on the earth.

Ode 1.5

by Horace
translated by John J. Trause

Quis multa gracilis te puer in rosa
perfusus liquidis urget odoribus
grato, Pyrrha, sub antro?
Cui flavam religas comam,

simplex munditiis? Heu quotiens fidem
mutatosque deos flebit et aspera
nigris aequora ventis
emirabitur insolens

qui nunc te fruitur credulus aurea,
qui semper vacuam, semper amabilem
sperat, nescius aurae
fallacis. Miseri, quibus

intemptata nites. Me tabula sacer
votiva paries indicat uvida
suspendisse potenti
vestimenta maris deo.

What slender boy, O Pyrrha, bathed in scents
Free-flowing, in the midst of many a rose
Beneath a pleasant grotto holds you close?

For whom do you bind back your golden hair
Simply exquisite in your sense of class?
How often will this one lament, alas,

Your infidelity and altered fate?
How often will he in his innocence
Be so amazed at your rough temperaments —

So rough with darker blasts —   this one who now
Enjoys you and believes you golden-fine,
Expects you to be always clear and kind,

Unmindful so of your deceitful airs?
O miserable are they to whom you shine
Untried. The sacred wall of this my shrine

With votive tablet indicates that I
Have also hung my garments ocean-steeped
To that almighty godhead of the deep.

*[previously published in **The Rift** vol. II, Issue 2
(Illuming, ©1998), published as "To A Flirt",
Adanna issue no. 3 (2013), **Trinacria** issue no. 10
(fall 2013)]*

To Poseidon Domatites

by Terence Ward

I sing to Poseidon Domatites, god of the house, the
doorways, the windows.
Builder of the walls of Troy, you bring safety and
protection to your own.
In the liminal spaces you dwell between sacred and
profane,
Purifying all that enters with your sacred waters.

Domatites, you stand between me and the fearful
unknown, and
you preserve the structure of my life against
formless dread.
Yet you bid me look upon my destruction and my
fear,
So that understanding brings acceptance.

Courter of the virgin Hestia, you stand at the
boundary,
Describing the proper place for honor to the gods.
Domatites, without you sacred spaces cannot stand
in my home
Or in my heart.

Kharin ekhoma soi.

Deep Beneath the Waves: Discovering Poseidon

by Michael Hardy

The sea is vast; from my earliest days it has held me
      close;
Your domain, Poseidon, though I knew you not in
      those times past.
The crashing waves send tendrils to caress the
      curious toes;
The sea is vast.

Miles deep, endlessly wide, your watery home held
      my thoughts fast.
I knew fish and whale, shell and clam, but of you no
      thought arose
As I read of current, reef and trench, and ships of
      steam or mast.

But now earth-shaker, horse-tamer, lord of the
      mighty ocean's throes,
I seek your ear and awesome gaze; I have heard
      your voice at last.
Praise the one whom sailors know, the god who
      calms the wind that blows.
The sea is vast.

Poseidon

by Cailin

Your scent ripples on the waves of time,
crashing down and pulling me back
to the first moment we shared.

You are the master of my memory,
mighty Poseidon —

your hair smells of seaweed and
wanderlust.
I drown in your perfume.

God of the Waves

by Mari

Hail Earth-shaker, god of the depths, of the crushing
weight of water countless fathoms from the sun.
Hail Poseidon the wave-tamer,
dark beard streaming in the sea winds;
Hail Triton's father,
Amphitrite's king.
He rides atop the cresting waves;
the ocean is his chariot.
The tides roar with their immeasurable strength —
with a gesture, he restrains the wrath of the deep.
His are the seas' bounties, riches past counting,
every good thing in the waves and shoals.
To Poseidon who soothes the sea,
we burn the incense,
sacrifice white bulls.
Where waves dash against sandy shores,
we burn our fatty offerings.
Tip out the aged wine;
pour it for the god.
We who live on his sufferance
find nothing too rich for the king
of the wild waters, the keeper of horses,
protector and overseer, Lord Poseidon:
he preserves our city; we live by his grace.
For the ancestor of waters,
for the father of bright-eyed nymphs,
we sing holy hymns,
we recite paeans.
Here on earth cradled by water,

praise the lord of seas, nurturer
of plants, tender of horses. Hail tempest lord,
sailors' reverence, hail to Poseidon of the depths.

Her Swells

by Mary Ann Back

Restraint is for the weak. Don't think, when you dip
your toes into the rhythmic swells of Amphitrite, I
won't swallow you whole, if it suits me. I am
Poseidon and her swells are mine. They rise and fall
with her every breath. They suckle my children and
soothe the storms that vex my soul. If man survives
her fickle fits, rest assured it is by my leave.

Should she cry, when misery churns her darkest
depths, no mortal man can stay my hand. My
judgment teems like a tempest tossed. No winds of
mercy blow. The foibles of man, laid bare, dash
upon the rocks of her weathered bones.

Her roiling currents, mountainous waves, and
swirling pools move as one with me. The rhythmic
swells of Amphitrite rise to meet my thrust. I am
Poseidon. And her swells are mine.

*[Originally published online through **Liquid
Imagination** in May 2012.]*

To Poseidon Dêlios

by Terence Ward

All honors are due to Poseidon Dêlios,
who raised the sacred island from the sea.
Without that holy place of sight
the world would lack prophecy.

Great god of the ocean foresaw
a failing of mortal thought:
that to externalize in law
would distinguish might from ought.

The insight that we lack
is within the gods, each one,
but none could make this clear
without a mortal tongue.

In Delos lay all hope
as Poseidon raised it high,
providing tools to ask the gods
of what and when and why.

Honored were you at that place
and honored should you be.
For now Apollon and great Zeus
bring truth through prophecy.

Invocation to Poseidon

by Frances Billinghurst

All hail to thee, Great God of the Seas
You who were known as Nethuns by the Etrusci
And venerated at Pylos and Thebes before all other
        Olympians,
And at Amnisos you were accompanied by the two
        queens, receiving many offerings.
All hail, Poseidon, Great God of the Seas.

All hail to thee, Great Protector of All
You who are the beloved of Amphritrite, the mother
        of Triton, dolphins and seals.
O, protector of many cities whose salted gift the
Athenians rejected, choosing Athena's fruiting olive
        instead.
Great calmer of the seas, to whom sailors call to
        guide their ships and fill their nets.
All hail, Poseidon, Great Protector of All.

All hail to thee, Great Shaker of the Earth
You who Plato declared chose dominion over
        Atlantis
Was it you who caused the collapse of Knossos with
        your mighty trident?
Were you not content with your watery realms? Did
        you long for Zeus's lofty abode or Hades
        darkened Underworld?

O, Creator of Islands, we know you are the greatest
        of all thine divine siblings.
All hail, Poseidon, Great Shaker of the Earth.

All hail to thee, Great Creator of Horses
You who ride upon your swift chariot drawn by the
        golden hippocampus of the sea
It was your name that charioteers revered from
        Anatolia through to Greece
As it was from your precious seed that magnificent
        beasts were formed.
You who tames the white horses that crash
        endlessly upon our shores
Reminding us constantly we are part of the cyclic
        nature of all things
All hail, Poseidon, Great Creator of Horses.

Poseidon Prayer Beads

by Jolene Dawe

Prayer beads are by no means a new concept, though I'm delighted to find more and more pagans talking about them: about making their own sets as well as sharing the many different ways they can be used. From Mala beads to Rosaries to Witches' Ladders, the use of beads as a tactile focal point is a concept that appeals to many.

I knew eight or nine years ago that I wanted a set of prayer beads for Poseidon. I knew I wanted to make them myself, and I knew that the number eight would be worked into the design. Beyond that, I hadn't a clue as to what I wanted, and so, I kept the idea on the back burner. I knew, in time, I'd find what I wanted. I had no idea it would take me almost a whole decade before the design came together with the materials.

So, here's my first bit of advice: if you want a prayer bead set right this minute, that's cool, but there's also nothing wrong with letting things take the time they take to come together. It all depends upon your wants, needs, and personality-type. I'm certainly more the sort to wait. With the exception of books (and, arguably, cats) (er, and also headscarves) I'm a bit of a minimalist. I don't like having a lot of *things*, and this includes spiritual tools. Since I'm also an animist (and as such, my tools are entities unto themselves) it just doesn't make sense to me to have a tool that I'm not going to value. So, throwing together any old beads onto a strand and fastening it to make a prayer bead set was not going to be the approach I took.

In 2014, a reread of *Walking the HeartRoad* by Silence Maestas (if you haven't read this book on devotional polytheism you really need to fix that) brought prayer beads back to the forefront of my mind. This reread happily coincided with our local Gem Faire show, and one thing after another fell into place, so that by the end of that weekend I finally, *finally* had my very own Poseidon prayer beads.

Construction
Things to Consider Before Construction

Deciding that you want to make your own set of prayer beads is only the first decision in this process. What materials do you want to use? Wood? Bone? Glass? Gemstone? Ceramic? Metal? Plastic? The sheer variety of bead types can be overwhelming. I knew going in that I didn't want to use gemstone, because most gemstones and I do not "get on." The ones I do get along with (rose quartz, amethyst, moonstone, flourite), while all very pretty, do not scream "Poseidon" to me. I wanted something that was evocative of the ocean, just at a glance — but since my personal taste in jewelry tends toward 'plain', I knew this was going to be difficult to manage. At long last I decided that I would opt for wooden beads, undyed, and that I'd simply use either two different sorts of woods, or two different sized beads, to differentiate between my eight focal beads and the spacers.

181*What colors do you want to use?* Different materials will have different options when it comes to colors, so knowing your color scheme going in is also important. Do you want your beads to be the same shape, even if they're not the same size? Do you want to include charms? Do you want the beads strung on beading wire, or on a cord, or worked onto chain? If you want it on beading wire, do you want a stretchy necklace or bracelet, or would you prefer one that clasps? Many beads out there come drilled with fairly small holes, so finding the right shapes and colors to fit on cord rather than beading wire can be tricky.

I knew going in that I wanted the number eight to be worked into the design. I was pretty sure that I wanted a bracelet rather than a necklace; I wanted something that I would actually use as intended, and I already have a nice assortment of devotional necklaces that I wear for Him. At the same time, I wasn't sure that I wanted a bracelet, either. I'm hard on my jewelry, and bracelets tend to suffer dire fates when upon my wrists. I wanted something that could stand up to frequent handling, that could be portable. I had this vague idea of having the beads wrapped around my wrist, loose enough to slip on and off without being on elastic, yet small enough that I could leave it on my wrist while commuting so my hands would be mostly free. I'd settled on wood as my material, and I knew I wanted some sort of focal charm to go with it.

I knew I wanted the prayer beads to be a conversation-starter. I wanted people to be able to look at them and become curious about them. While

I don't believe for one minute that Poseidon needs my help in drawing people to Him, I'd be lying if I said I don't like talking about Him, talking about being a devotee of His, or talking about how our gods are very much alive and present in our lives. I think it's important to live our faiths out loud when we can, because so many people cannot. I can, and so I feel it's part of my path to do so, and I wanted these prayer beads to look enough like prayer beads that, while in use they were obviously prayer beads, but eye-catching enough that people might say, "Wait, what?" and maybe ask me questions. (Yes. I made mine with an eye toward being interrupted in prayer while praying out and about.)

As you go shopping for the materials that will become your prayer beads, remember to also keep an open mind — and to keep an eye open for inspiration. Because shopping can be overwhelming for me, I tend to put mental blinders on. Once I decided I was going to get wooden beads, all I looked at were wooden beads, and as a result I wasn't finding a contrast in color that I wanted …. Until one booth caught my eye. Sitting on a table, nestled in a sea of various gemstones, were some strands of quartz beads treated in such a way that they looked like the ocean caught into bead form. The way the light caught the glass brought to mind sunlight bouncing back up from the murky depths. It conjured up time spent out at sea, without land in sight. *This*. *This* was the bead I'd been waiting for. (Despite that, it wasn't until I'd walked by the booth a third time to admire the beads that my partner decided enough was enough already and made me purchase them. Don't be like me. Don't be so set in your ways that you're not open to changing your plan if something perfect presents itself.)

Since these are going to be devotional tools, another thing to consider is: how are you going to consecrate the prayer beads? Do you want to line up the construction with a particular moon phase or time of day? Will you smudge the item? Will you leave it out under the moon or sun to bask in the celestial energies? This can be as customized to your practice and your beliefs as you want to make it be — there is no right or wrong, here.

Once mine were completed, I spritzed them with the holy water that I make, which is a combination of waters from several nearby sources (Pacific ocean water, rainwater, snow- and/or hail-melt, a few drops from Crater Lake, and river water gathered from both the Willamette and the MacKenzie rivers, blended in a glass jar that I leave out under the full moon every month. Yes, there's a theme.) I would have done more than spritzed them if I hadn't used wood beads, and in hindsight I wish I had thought to soak the glass before constructing the bracelet. You can do whatever it is that you want to do to dedicate your beads to this goal — providing that the material you've used can stand up to it.

What you'll need for constructing your prayer beads. The beads that you've picked out to use (I used eight 10mm quartz beads as my focal beads, and twenty 8mm wooden beads as my spacers).

The wire or cord you want to use. (I used a 49-strand professional quality Accuflex beading wire, which is a clear-coated stainless steel because I am an extreme klutz with my bracelets, but there are many sorts of wire available on the market)

Any focal charm or bead you might want to use. (I used an antiqued bronze octopus charm that Beth had in stock) (The perks of living with a professional jeweler!)

Any tools or pieces that may be necessary for assemblage. (Because I put mine on non-stretchy wire, I needed crimps and crimping tools to attach the wire to the focal charm. If I'd wanted this to clasp on my wrist I would have needed the clasp and O-ring as well)

A beading board is not strictly necessary, but it can make beading so much easier, and can be worth the $5-7 investment.

If you don't have any of these tools, or if you feel your ability isn't up to snuff when it comes to the finer details of constructing jewelry and you *don't* have a live-in professional jeweler) find a friend who has some beading experience, or visit a local craft or beading store. Especially with the beading stores, many offer use of their beading tools so long as you purchase your beads and findings and wire with them.

Using Your Prayer Beads

This is my favorite part, because how you use your prayer beads is *entirely* up to you! You can write up your own prayer to use. You can adapt a poem or a prayer that already exists to suit your needs. You can simply hold them in your hands while you meditate, letting your mind focus on your god, your spirit, your relationship.

For myself, I know that I tend to be extremely informal when it comes to prayers and praying. Half the time I don't even use words. Still, part of what intrigued me about prayer beads was this idea of having a formal prayer memorized. Having a specific set of prayers said in specific order — I think there's something to be said for that. Having something to recite by rote can help on the days when you are overwhelmed or hard pressed for time or are ill or distracted. Having a standing act of devotion (it need not be prayer beads) is like having a well-worn path to your destination. All level ground, no surprises, no uphill trek. When you are down and out, when you need solace and comfort, when all your fight is going into some other area of your life, being able to touch in with your gods and spirits with ease is something that cannot be discounted. I wanted something that could touch upon the eight most important aspects of Poseidon as they correspond to my relationship with Him, whether it be a function He fulfills, a cause that is important to u/Us, or a historical association that matters to Him.

Because I have a bad habit of over-thinking and over-complicating things (in an effort to make it 'perfect') I hesitated putting this into writing for longer than I ought to have, after the beads were completed, because I was still warring within myself over the form: if it's to be formal, shouldn't the names be Hellenic? If I'm talking about

185

Poseidon as my foundation, shouldn't it be Poseidon Domatites? It is, at times, but I'm not uniform with how I approach this. I'm a native English speaker; I use English in my worship. I find value exploring outside of my native tongue, but that's a mental exercise that I didn't necessarily want for my ' go to' prayer for my prayer beads. What I have written down is:

Hail, Compassionate Poseidon,
Lord of healing, of empathy, of love,
I praise You.

Hail, Rainmaker Poseidon,
Lord of growth, nourishing god,
I praise You.

Hail, Poseidon Taureos,
Lord of the beasts, thundering one, roaring one,
I praise You.

Hail, Shaker of the Earth,
Deep-reaching, dark-dwelling, secret-keeping,
I praise You.

Hail, Poseidon Hippios,
Lord of Horses, fierce stallion, wild god,
I praise You.

Hail, Poseidon Domatites,
Lord of my hearth, center to my heart, my
        foundation,
I praise You.

Hail, Poseidon Asphaleios,
Patient Lord, understanding god, generous one,
I praise You.

Hail Poseidon Basileus,
my Lord, my King, my God,
I praise You.

Now, in the interest of full disclosure — I love this prayer. It's personal, it's rooted in my history of worshiping Poseidon and how o/Our relationship has grown over time. It brings in bits of that history that I love (viewing Him as my Hearth, my center, from the beginning, and then finding an historical precedence for connecting Poseidon with the foundations of a dwelling, for example), but it also brings in bits of our history that can be uncomfortable (naming Him king, for example. I don't know why, still, I have such a hard time standing before His Shrine and naming Him King, when I don't have a hard time calling Odin King, and I have no problem calling Poseidon 'Lord' or 'God'. I don't know what it is about 'King' that makes me uncomfortable ... so I name Him thus in defiance of emotions that don't make sense/I don't understand, in hopes to eventually come to grips with them). I love its mix-mashy-ness, I love its nod toward historical references followed by completely modern and private-to-me references. I love this prayer.

But I don't use it as much as I use another one. It's a simple song/chant thing that I wrote for

Him right before I gave Him my vows. It's a simple plea: *Poseidon, surround me with Your love. Poseidon, surround me with Your strength*. Over and over and over again. I run my hands over the beads as I go, counting my way. It's not pretty, it's not fancy, but the sound of this plea being chanted combined with rhythmic touch of the beads under my fingers brings me into a space of worship that involves not just sound, but also touch. It brings my body into the act of prayer as much as it brings my mind into it, so much so that at times, I forget about both of them entirely, and there is just … Poseidon.

It's not always like that — I'd even say that it's mostly not like that. Transcendence. Mostly it's sitting (or walking, or whatever) and reciting, and running my hands over the beads, all eight, and then the charm, and then again, and then again. And that brings its own benefits, as well.

In the interest of further disclosure? I broke my charm, about two months after having constructed the beads. I decided I wanted to carry them in my pocket while at work, and one of the tentacles on the octopus snapped off. I hadn't anticipated wanting to have them on my person so much; I didn't anticipate how much the simple act of holding them would 'set me in the mood' to carry my god further into my day. I've been devoted to Him for nearly twenty years as of this writing, and living with my life centered around my devotion to Him for over eleven; surely I was already 'devoted enough'?

This was a great reminder that there is never an end to how we can grow closer to our gods, that there's no journey's end, here, just that journey. It was also a needed reminder that experiential knowledge is sometimes more valuable than intellectual knowledge. Since I love the look of this set, I don't want to switch the focal charm to something less fragile; therefore I've decided to not carry it around in my pocket anymore. Hopefully the second charm will live longer.

I mention this to highlight: if you're thinking about making your own set, how you plan to use them and wear them should inform your choice of beads and charms. Delicately armed octopuses, for example, do not survive bending and twisting and stretching and frequent movement. Something to keep in mind.

Prayer beads are a wonderful, powerful addition to our tools of worship and devotion. I encourage anyone even remotely interested to make a set, or have someone make you a set, or adopt a string of beads already made and write prayers to them. Going off the cuff with the prayers is okay — I'm all for improvisational prayers — but even if you're like me, and less inclined toward the formal, I encourage you to create a prayer that you stick to, at least for a while, simply to experience what doing so can offer you and your practice. Like me, you might "know" that that isn't your style, that you prefer praying from your gut and your heart, and less from your brain. If I had stuck with what I "knew" about myself, I would not have experienced the benefits that developing a prayer set, a prayer to go along with it, and a routine with how to recite the prayer, gave me.

Poseidon, He continually prods, coaxes, shoves, and encourages me to places outside my comfort zones. What a curious, wise, generous, wonderful god, this god. Hail, hail, O Compassionate One.

Poseidon:
Designed to Care

by Bella Michel

I am god of the ocean
and I am tired of the seashells.
They lay and crackle underneath my feet.
There are sands and the grooves of the floor
the potholes that bubble and croak,
      and the music
of the deep wet world beneath.
I once thought all of this, beautiful.

I've been Designed to Care for the life in the great
      beneath;
for all of the sirens of the seas
who lure me to sleep; singing
and bring me into the caves
underneath the shores.

Still, I know I will not sleep tonight
All I can think about
Is a young girl; drowned.
I think it strange that I'm finding myself solemn.
Whatever has become of me?

I saw a mortal man: sailing;
He lost his daughter, Rosaline.
She hit my waters: a wild sea
and I did nothing to help her breathe.

I listened to her pulse slow;
the lights of her eyes, dimmed low.
What became of her barren of body?:
Oh I should know.
They were just bones.

And I think if I had bones: if I was not just Faith
        and true power
That I would be crying, and tearing through the
        tides
Just to save her; that beautiful girl.

But I have to be the god here; the harsh spear.
I must do this alone; be sad of death.
It's because the sirens are filthy, and I know,
that they will never understand.

They will sing songs of mockery
and ease me to sleep with their haunting, sweet
        sounds:
Teasing me with "un-death."
They will remind me, through and through,
that I will never join her.
I can never die.

As I walk below the waters, just above the
        underworld, I wonder:
Is there ever a day I might be undone?: Unraveled,
        like the mortal?

192

Can I never turn to dust and just become one with
    the earth?

I know I should not be jealous of life in motion:
even as bodies and spirits die.

Yet it's unsettling when I saw her breath;
A gasp for air and a tremble in fear.
Right then, I knew,
I wanted to die right along with her;
That I want to die right alongside her.
Now
I wish my breath could stop.
It would be a wonderful thing to, one day, just stop
    breathing.

I keep thinking, "why? Why have I come to believe
    this?"
But the answer is here.
The thoughts slam against the shores of mind.
It hits me that: "perhaps," I think, "I loved a mortal
    soul."

Poseidon Acrostic

by Melia Brokaw

Port Master
Of horses
Sea king
Earth Holder
Isthmian games honoree
Daimon of Water
Orion's Father
Neptune

To Poseidon Erechtheus

by Terence Ward

Hail, Poseidon, and hear my words,
as I sing praises to you as Erechtheus.
Beloved of Athens you are,
that jewel of my ancestors.

The Athenians thought long and hard
before giving the city's patronage to mighty Athena.
They weighed her gift of olives
against the spring you summoned forth.

Blessed indeed were they to have such a spring!
For while grey-eyed Athena received the honor,
it was the salty brine which preserved that fruit
and transformed the way nourishment was shared.

To you was given a temple straddling unstable lands
and the Athenians traced their heritage back to you.
Erechtheus, from you sprang the elements of
      civilization,
and for that alone I praise and honor you.

Hymn to Poseidon, Lord of Polluted Waters

by Rebecca Buchanan

Hail Poseidon
Lord of Polluted Waters
Lord of the Global Garbage Dump
Lord of Over-Fished Seas and Bloody Whales
Hail Poseidon
Lord of Dying Oceans

Prayer to Poseidon for the Protection of His Children

by Natasha Handy

I call to Poseidon, great god of the seas,
fond husband of ocean-dwelling Amphitrite,
son of ancient Kronos and wild-hearted Rhea:
I beseech you this day/night to come forth and bear
witness to my rite and heed my warning.

Your waters are being polluted
and the children of your realm are being persecuted
        near to extinction,
especially those sea creatures that you hold dear to
        your heart.
In this I beseech you to hold aloft your trident in
        rage
and strike down those who do your children harm
for the sake of their own benefit —
for it is those sailors and fishermen who are the
cause of the injustice inflicted upon your children.

Dark-haired Poseidon, the waters of the world obey
        you,
those briny depths that brought us all into life.
Poseidon, maker and master of horses, trident-
        bearer,
earth-shaker, lord of the beasts of the deep,
        lord of the thrashing waves, sea-god:
show those who do your creatures harm no mercy.

Hail Poseidon!

by Frances Billinghurst

The amount of sea pollution is horrendous. The old adage "out of mind, out of sight" seems to occur while out in the middle of the ocean where it appears to be okay to throw rubbish overboard so that it becomes someone else's problem. That "someone" is usually the marine inhabitants. They (experts) say that there is an "island" of rubbish somewhere in the Pacific Ocean that is at least the size of the American state of Texas (some 700,000 square kilometres), possibly larger, yet no one seems to care.

This ritual calls upon Poseidon, the Greek God of the sea and the protector of the waters, and requests his protection to all those creatures of the seas and oceans whose habitats are being polluted and whose lives are placed in danger from mankind's disregard and sheer laziness.

Brief Background to Poseidon

According to ancient Greek myth, Poseidon was the brother of Zeus and Hades between whom, after their farther Kronos was overthrown, the three realms were divided – Zeus, the heavens; Hades the Underworld, and Poseidon, the sea. He was also considered to be the God who ruled over the rivers, floods and droughts, as well as earthquakes and horses. Depicted as a sturdy built mature man, Poseidon often carried his trident from which earthquakes would be created when touched the ground which earnt him the epithet of "earth shaker." His sacred day was the 8th of each month.

Poseidon was married to Amphiatrite, the granddaughter of the Titan Oceanus (unending stream of water encircling the world), and was associated with various other Goddesses. When he lusted after Demeter, she distracted his advances by asking him to create the most beautiful animal that the world had ever seen – the result of which was the first horse by which time his lust for Demeter had subsided. Another myth recalls Demeter turning herself into a mare and attempting to blend in with a herd of horses to avoid Poseidon's attention. However, he took on the form of a stallion and mated with her, the result was a horse, Arion which was capable of human speech.

Poseidon lost to Athena to have the city of Athens names after him when the spring from his trident resulted in salty water as opposed to Athena's gift of olives. He was honoured by seafarers and charioteers.

Items Needed

- Image or statue of Poseidon (alternatively symbols of the sea including seashells, pebbles, sand can be used)

- Altar cloth of blue/sea colour or with a sea print
- Incense: Myrrh
- Bowl of salt water (either from the sea or water to which salt has been added)
- Candle – preferably sea blue (teal, green/blue)
- Blessing Oil (3 drops Palmarosa, 2 drops Ylang-ylang and 1 drop Jasmine). Saltwater can be used as an alternative
- Offering – can be organic (if thrown into the ocean or left on the altar) or another form[1]

Preparation

If possible, this rite should be performed at the shoreline or at the edge of a body of water (lake, river, stream) etc. If this is not possible, ensure that you have a picture of the ocean as the focal point within your working area, along with image pertaining to the sea – seabirds, seashells, even the "rubbish" island. Such images can be drawn or downloaded from the internet. It is recommended to write Poseidon's name on the sand to ensure that he knows that the altar is for him.

---

[1] Within ancient Greek culture, there were two types of offerings that were made to their Gods: (a) *Votive offerings* occurred when a deal was struck between the worshipper and the deity whereby the votive offering was the agreed amount promises (ie, 10% of goods if ship arrives safely in harbour whereby a statue to the equivalent of that value was made in honour of the deity); or (b) *Thank offerings* which referred to all other kinds of offerings left at the altar in honour of deity as an expression of gratitude.

If you are at the shoreline or the edge of a body of water, setting up a formal circle, calling the quarters etc is not necessary. However, if you wish to do this, then do so – ensuring that the ritual is performed within this sacred space.

The altar can be made from a blue/sea coloured cloth or cloth with a sea print placed on the ground, upon which an image/statue of Poseidon is placed. Alternatively, in the centre of the sacred space on a bowl, place the statue of Poseidon upon blue glass beads so that the statue is raised. Pour water around the base of the statue in the bowl. If at the beach, write Poseidon's name (or draw a symbol that relates to him, i.e. the trident) to ensure that the God knows that this rite is for him.

Commencement of Rite

If performed as a solitary, purify self prior to entering the ritual area by asperging with water, smudging with incense and anointing self with a blessing oil (made from ingredients given above). If rite is performed with other participates, each participant may be anointed by stepping through a container of water, before being smudged and anointed.

Acknowledgment/Statement of Intent

I declare that the purpose of this rite is to call for Poseidon's protection of all his inhabitants in and around his watery abode from the actions and the results of such actions stemming from mankind's disregard towards other species, especially those who reside in the watery abodes.

May we be reminded that as humans, we should act as care-takers of this planet and its finite resources, that such resources serve all beyond our selves, and as such, the mindless dumping of unwanted waste into Poseidon's sacred abode must cease.

All hail, Soter Poseidon, all hail. (*call and response*)[2]

Creating Sacred Space

Circumbrate the space three times with salt water, candle and incense:

By the power of this blessed water and in Poseidon's name, I bless this space.
All hail, Soter Poseidon, all hail. (*call and response*)

By the power of this sacred flame and in Poseidon's name, I bless this space.
All hail, Soter Poseidon, all hail. (*call and response*)

[2] If this rite is being conducted solitary, the call and response prompts need not apply.

By the power of this holy scent and in Poseidon's name, I bless this space.

All hail, Soter Poseidon, all hail. (*call and response*)

Evocation to Poseidon[3]

I begin to sing about Poseidon, the great God,
Shaker-of-the-Land and of the sea unharvested;
God of the deep who holdeth Helicon and wide Aegae.
A double meed of honour have the gods given thee,
O Shaker of the Earth, to be a tamer of horses and a saviour of ships
Hail, Prince, thou girdler of the Earth, thou dark-haired God, and with kindly heart,
O blessed one, do thou befriend the mariners.

Hail, O Mighty Bull of the Sea (*call and response*)

We sing praises to you, O Mighty Poseidon (*call and response*)

Master of the waves and the hidden depths

---

[3] Adapted from the "Homeric Hymn to Poseidon" (translated by Evelyn-White)

Guardian and protector of all who reside
On and within your watery realm.
Wild horses ride your bitter brine
Only to crash endlessly against the shore
Your voice booms up from the depths

Hail, O Mighty Shaker of the Earth (*call and response*)

We sing praises to you, O Mighty Poseidon (*call and response*)

Earth-shaker, loudest voice
In the world between heaven and underworld,
The voice that booms up from the depths
Of every water-borne soul.

Hail, O Mighty Giver of horses and of ships (*call and response*)

We sing praises to you, O Mighty Poseidon (*call and response*)

Orphic Hymn XVII (To Poseidon)[4]

Hear, Poseidon, ruler of the sea profound,
whose liquid grasp begirds the solid ground;
who, at the bottom of the stormy main,

---

[4] Orphic Hymn XVII (translated by Thomas Taylor) (http://www.theoi.com/Text/OrphicHymns1.html#16)

dark and deep-bosomed holdest they watery
reign.
Thy awful hand the brazen trident bears,
and sea's utmost bound thy will reveres.
Thee I invoke, whose steeds the foam divide,
from whose dark locks the briny waters glide;

shoe voice, loud sounding through the roaring
deep,
drives all its billows in a raging heap;
when fiercely riding through the boiling sea,
thy hoarse command the trembling waves
obey.
Earth-shaking, dark-haired God, the liquid
plains,
the third division, fate to thee ordains.
'Tis thine, cerulean daimon, to survey,
well-pleased, the monsters of the ocean play.

Confirm earth's basis, and with prosperous
gales
waft ships along, and swell the spacious sails;
add gentle peace, and fair-haired health
beside,
and pour abundance in a blameless tide.

Participant is asperged with salt water with
the left over water being poured as a libation.

And as Theseus cursed his son by Poseidon's breath that he shall fall swiftly to the horse of Death, Hippolytos reached the Gulf of Saronis when:

> Just there an angry sound,
> Slow swelling, like God's thunder underground,
> Broke on us, and we trembled. And the steeds
> Pricked their ears skyward, and threw back their heads
> And wonder came on all men, and affright,
> Whence rose that awful voice? And swift our sight
> Turned seaward, down the salt and roaring sand.

A great wave rose and swept towards the chariot of Hippolytos, and:

> Three lines of wave together raced, and, full
> In the white crest of them, a wild Sea-Bull
> Flung to the shore, a fell and marvellous Thing.
> The whole land held his voice, and answering
> Roared in each echo.

O Mighty Bull of the Sea
Protect those creatures who take refuge in
your watery abode
From mankind's disregard and lack of respect.
Remind us that all life is sacred
And for us to continue reaping your generous
bounty
We must be grateful, show more humility as
all life is connected.

All hail, Soter Poseidon, all hail. (*call and
response*)[5]

Chant

Earth-Shaker, Storm Maker
Bull of the Sea
God of the Deep, Horses Keep
All praise to thee.

Chant is repeated until a trance-like state is
achieved. Participant then enter into private
communication with the God, preferably asking for
his protection over the oceans and of all creatures
that inhabit them.

---

[5] Based on *Myths of Greece and Rome* by Jane Harrison (1928)
(http://www.sacred-texts.com/cla/mgr/mgr12.htm)

Closing

Although the sacred space being utilised was marked out and cleansed, no formal circle casting was undertaken, therefore the banishing of such is not necessary. If the rite is to be performed at the water's edge, organic offerings can be relinquished into the body of water. If inside, offerings should be placed on the altar where they remain or placed outside to disintegrate naturally. If the offering is votive in nature, then a donation to a suitable charity or other such organisation should be made as soon as the participant is able to.

To Poseidon

by Amanda Sioux Blake

The Earth-Shaker inhales
And the tides come in
The Holder of Earth exhales
And the tides go out

O Poseidon, you are the mightiest of the
Olympians!
Your realm extends to cover three-fourths of the
world
The only part of our planet still mysterious to man
Unknown, Unpenetrated,
Is the dark world beneath your waves.

Briny One of seaweed beard
What secrets do you hold?
You eyes are swirling pools of azure
You are the mighty, the terrible
And the merciful, the rescuer of lost sailors
You are the lover of Gaia
And earthy Demeter

To Poseidon Mousêgetês

by Terence Ward

A song never sung goes to Poseidon Mousêgetês,
for memory flees and with it, this name.
Leader of Muses before they gave beauty voice,
guardian of the soft heart that through poetry,
      weeps.
When the brothers divided the sky from the land,
and each took a portion, his own to command,
dark Haides withdrew to the places unseen,
while above sat the throne of Zeus Celestine.
Sea from sky, earth from under,
some divisions were clear,
less so for those spirits
not of this world, but near.
Some flocked to Haides, of money and death.
To Zeus clove spirits of justice and breath.
And closest to the lands that mortals eyes beheld
were the daimones of beauty, encased in hard shells.
So precious did he find them,
these daimones, bright and pure,
that Poseidon loathed to risk them
near his sacred, rocky shores.
In time, the young god knew
that this world was yet unborn
as he watched the first men's races,
lived not with love, but scorn.
With each new god that came
to add richness to the world,

Poseidon let the shells dissolve
until beauty was unfurled.
And into that potential
did his brother in the sky
seek several kind goddesses
with which, in time, to lie.
Mousêgetês is not your name
for those maidens were unknown
until you freed potential
so that artist could carve stone.

Prayer to Poseidon Soter

by Ann Hatzakis

Sea-Father and Lord of Horses
We Thank you for your protection
in the season of storms
Ruler of both deep and shallow seas
Grant to us all your grace
Help us maintain health, peace and prosperity
And all good things, so that we may
Praise you now and at a future date.

Sea of Dissimilitude:
Poseidon and Platonism

by Edward P. Butler

The foundation of the Platonic philosophical inquiry into the nature of Poseidon is the mythic structure of the three-way division of Kronos' sovereignty between his sons Zeus, Poseidon and Hades (*Iliad* 15.187-193), which Plato at *Gorgias* 523a has Socrates state to be a doctrine (*logos*) of the first importance. "In three ways have all things been divided," Poseidon says,

> and to each has been apportioned his domain. I indeed, when the lots were shaken, was allotted the gray sea to be my home forever, and Hades the murky darkness, while Zeus was allotted the broad heaven in the air and the clouds; but the Earth and blessed Olympus still remain common to all. (Trans. Murray and Wyatt, modified)

The Platonic interpretation of this division is governed by the statement in the *Iliad* text that it constitutes a division of all things (*panta*, 189). Therefore, it cannot be treated merely as a division according to the bare natural sense of these terms — the sea, the darkness, the heavens. Rather, these symbols must encompass their literal referents, but also far more. As the Platonist Proclus explains, the division into what Homer refers to as *timai* (189), 'honors' or prerogatives, or of what Plato characterizes as the Kronian *archê*, 'authority' — which in the sense of 'principle' is also a basic philosophical term for Platonists and other Hellenic philosophers — "designates the providence [*pronoia*] divided into three" by the sons of Kronos (*PT* 6.8.35.15-17).[1] *Pronoia*, 'providence', is, as its name denotes, pre-intelligence, which for Platonists means the domain prior to Intellect, *Nous*:

> Providence, then, resides primarily in the Gods. For indeed, where should an activity prior to Intellect be found, if not in those who are above Being [lit. 'supra-essential', *hyperousios*]? ... In virtue of their being, then, and in virtue of being excellences [*agathotêtes*, 'supreme goodnesses'], the Gods exercise providence towards all things, filling all with a goodness which is prior to Intellect. (Proclus, *ET* prop. 120, trans. Dodds, mod.)[2]

Every God, *qua* God, exercises providence toward all things (*ET* prop. 134). Providence, then, is always a way of dividing all things, rather than being itself a portion. The providence exercised by each deity expresses that deity's direct relationship, not to some discrete domain of things over which they have been given charge, but to everything. Every deity in this way relates directly to everything. The division of Kronos' authority among his sons, therefore, insofar as it is really a

214

division of providence, must result in three portions each of which is yet in some sense the Totality. This is the sense in which we must try to understand Poseidon's 'portion': dynamically, that is, as a measure of all things (cf. Proclus, *PT* 6.8.41.3, "the measures of providence"; *ET* prop. 117: "Every God is a measure of things existent").

The three sons of Kronos are understood by Platonists as demiurges, that is, 'artisans', crafting the universe at all times. In an initial adumbration of the division, Proclus states that "among the three demiurges, the first [Zeus] is the cause for encosmic beings of stable institution, the second [Poseidon] of generation proceeding to all, the third [Hades] of circling back upon the principle," (*PT* 6.8.42.24-27). This differentiation of causality corresponds to the general Platonic structure of being: beings remain in themselves, proceed into nonidentity with themselves, and return to the principles that constitute them. The three sons of Kronos thus effectively operate these three motions of being on behalf of the whole cosmos. A little later, Proclus states that "the allotment and distribution of them ... is according to the whole universe, the first of them [Zeus] producing essences [or 'substances', *ousiai*], the second [Poseidon] lives and generations [*geneseis*, processes of coming-to-be], and the third [Hades] administering formal divisions," (46.2-5). This division, unlike the former, which was by modes of causality, is by the products of causality: Zeus produces all things insofar as they are substances or dependencies of substances, Poseidon produces all things insofar as they are alive or dependencies of living things, and Hades produces all things insofar as they are forms or dependencies of forms. These methods of division all apply to the totality itself; by contrast, "according to the parts of the all" Zeus governs the sphere of the fixed stars, Poseidon "directs the planetary region and renders efficacious and fecund the multiform movements in it," while Hades administers the sublunary world (46.8-14). We can see from this that even when the Platonist matches the divisions of the Kronian sovereignty to parts of the cosmos, the partitions are very different than what a literal reading would expect. In a further elaboration of Poseidon's sphere of action, this time according to an elemental division, Proclus accords to Zeus the aetheric and fiery, while Poseidon "moves in every way the intermediary and constantly changing elements and presides over the humid substance found in both air and water," and Hades governs earth (46.16-23).

Even once through the analysis of Poseidon's activity we arrive at the physical element of water, then, its role relative to Poseidon is as medium of his power of motion. Water itself as a physical element is for the Platonist just a tangible part of a much wider system. Hence, in a discussion of Okeanos in his *Timaeus* commentary, Proclus explains that Okeanos everywhere distinguishes first from second orders ... is the cause of motion, procession and power ... in the Gods ... imparts a kinetic and providential causality ... subsists in each of the elements ... in the case of chthonic orders, zoogonic and demiurgic, distinguishing them, of powers connective of the productive principles [*logoi*] of the Earth [Gê] and overseers [*ephoroi*] of generation, awakening them, multiplying them and calling them forth into motion. (*IT* 3.178-9)[3]

Okeanos, then, who is, we must remember, the source of fresh water in nature, fulfills this function as part of a broader project, a kind of connecting, separating and fructifying medium of all motion, beginning with the ideal 'motion' existing among the Gods themselves. Again, Proclus speaks of Okeanos as "generating all motion collectively, whether divine or intellective or psychical or physical," (ibid., 179) while his partner Tethys "is the cause of all the separation of the streams [*ochetoi*] proceeding from Okeanos" (180), by which Proclus means the ten species of motion Plato identifies in the *Laws* (894c-d).

A further aspect of the division of the Kronian sovereignty presented by Homer at *Iliad* 15.187ff is suggested by Damascius, who in his commentary on Plato's *Phaedo* (II §131) remarks that, inasmuch as Poseidon himself is the speaker in this passage, he "divides his own realm," i.e., the realm of genesis or generation, and thus refers, in effect, to the heavenly portion of that domain as accorded to Zeus and the chthonic portion of it to Hades. Proclus seems to concur, remarking in his *Timaeus* commentary (1.272) that some "call the summits of generation heaven," and proceeds to quote *Iliad* 15.192, "Zeus was allotted the broad heaven in the air and the clouds," which must, after all, to refer to something distinct from Olympos, which the Homeric passage says, like Earth, remains "common to all". Damascius elaborates, speculating that "if instead of Poseidon ... the speaker were Zeus, he would no doubt have divided heaven into three ... giving himself the sphere of the fixed stars, Poseidon the sphere down to the sun, and the rest to Pluto." The Earth, too, Damascius says, would be subject to a similar division "into a celestial, a terrestrial, and a median region; there is worship of Olympian Earth and Chthonic Earth, and an intermediate one may consequently be inferred."[4] According to Plutarch, "Olympian Earth" is a name for the Moon (*De def. orac.* 416e), and therefore this would be the Zeusian portion, so to speak, of Hades' domain. In these internal divisions of the three demiurges' realms we see an example of what I have termed "polycentric polytheism", in a form frequently attested among the Platonists, in which there is said to be, e.g., a Zeus and a Hades "in" Poseidon, and vice versa. Thus, elsewhere in Damascius' *Phaedo* commentary (I §483), Damascius speaks of Hades using "the

Zeusian or Poseidonian *idion* of himself" to send souls upwards from the place of judgment to the palace of Zeus, or down again into Poseidon's realm of genesis. Hence, the Zeus who would be apportioned the Moon as "Olympian Earth" in the division as it would be 'spoken' by Hades would be the Zeus in Hades, Hades' Zeusian 'idiom' or other self.

The sovereignty divided up among the sons of Kronos is itself, however, only one of several distinct sovereignties exercised within Hellenic theology. One of the important features of the sovereignty Poseidon exercises, in fact, is its special relationship, through Okeanos, to the sovereignty of Ouranos, which encompasses the sovereignties of Kronos and of Zeus alike. Basing himself on the tradition we know primarily from Apollodorus' *Bibliotheca* (1.1.4) according to which Okeanos, alone of the children of Ouranos, did not participate in the castration of his father, Proclus explains that Okeanos

> both remains and proceeds, uniting himself to his father, and not departing from his kingdom. But the rest, rejoicing in procession, are said to have fulfilled the will [*boulêsis*] of Gê, and to have plotted against their father, dividing themselves from his kingdom and proceeding into a different order [*diakosmêsis*] … Okeanos prohibited them from obeying the mandates of

their mother, being in doubt concerning the action [*praxis*]. (*IT* 3.185)

Okeanos resists the definitive separation of the discrete realms of the cosmos that follows from putting Gê's will into practice, and by this act of reserve sustains in himself the Ouranian sovereignty, his own realm being an extension of Ouranian sovereignty. Drawing on Orphic tradition, Proclus says that Okeanos "dwells in the divine streams posterior to Olympos, and treats with the Ouranos which is there, and not the highest Ouranos, but as the myth says, the one which fell from Olympos, and was there arranged," (ibid., 186). As a result, whereas in the intellective order, Kronos is above Okeanos, "for in that order the causes of intellection are stronger than those of motion, but here, on the contrary, all things are changing and flowing, so that here Okeanos is appropriately prior to Kronos, being the source [lit. 'fountain', *pêgê*] of motion," (187). Poseidon, by comparison, is said to be the demiurge "governing particularly the psychical order, for he is the God who is the cause of motion and of all generation, and the psyche is the first of generated natures and is motion with respect to its substance," (*PT* 6.22.97.12-15).

Proclus' immediate concern in the passage on Okeanos from the *Timaeus* commentary is to harmonize the account that makes Kronos and Rhea, not the siblings of Okeanos, as in Hesiod, but the children of Okeanos and Tethys; but it also has the effect of affirming an alternate sovereignty of motion with profound consequences for the sovereignty Poseidon exercises within the Olympian order, insofar as this Ouranian sovereignty retained by Okeanos is delivered, in effect, directly into Poseidon's hands, though not solely into his. We must also take Hera into account in this respect, because in the Platonic interpretation of Hellenic theology she presides over motion, *kinêsis*, from the intellective plane and in the closest cooperation with Zeus' demiurgic project.[5] This in turn sheds light, however, upon the cooperation between Hera and Poseidon in the uprising against Zeus mentioned by Homer (*Iliad* 1.399-400), which also includes Athena, who as granddaughter of Okeanos through her mother Mêtis could be seen to partake as well in the alternate, Ouranian sovereignty. Above all, we may regard Aphrodite, who clearly exercises an undisputed power over Zeus, and who is the daughter of Ouranos via the medium of Pontos, the sea, into whom the severed genitals of Ouranos fall, as the highest embodiment of this primordial authority, as befits Aphrodite's role, for example, as sole demiurge in Empedocles' philosophical-theological cosmogony. The power of an intellective order with soul, love, and flux at its center rather than mind and form is certainly recognized by Plato at numerous points throughout his work, and clearly constitutes for him the primary rival to the Zeus-centered order he labors to establish. Thus, while the philosophical position Plato advocates is under the patronage of Zeus (*Phaedrus* 252e), the position Plato associates with Heraclitus, namely that "all things move and nothing abides," and that being is like "a river, and one cannot step into the same river twice," he also identifies with Homer's characterization of Okeanos and Tethys as those "from whom the Gods are sprung" (*Cratylus* 402a-c; *Iliad* 14.201). Plato states this thesis in more sweeping terms in his *Theaetetus*:

> on this subject all the philosophers except Parmenides may be classified together — Protagoras and Heraclitus and Empedocles — as well as the chief poets in the two kinds of poetry, Epicharmus in comedy and in tragedy Homer, who, in saying "Okeanos from whom the Gods are sprung, and Tethys their mother," has said that all things are the offspring of flux and of motion. (*Theaetetus* 152e)

Given the abundant differences between these diverse philosophical, sophistic and poetic worldviews, what is it that ultimately secures the ideological integrity of them, allowing Plato to determine them through the universal formula that "it is out of movement and motion and mixture with one another that all those things become which we wrongly say 'are' — wrongly, because nothing ever is, but is always becoming," (152d, trans. H. N.

Fowler)? From the perspective of the accomplished Platonic system, the answer is the theological truth of a widespread divine authority distinct from that of Zeus, not opposed to his reign, but compelling in its own right throughout the Hellenic theological-cultural field.[6]

The occasion for most of Proclus' remarks about Poseidon is Plato's account of the city-state of Atlantis, from the *Timaeus* and the *Critias*. Atlantis is allotted to Poseidon, where he settles the children begotten by him upon a mortal woman, Cleito (*Critias* 113b-d). The polity of Atlantis is important for Proclus for its structural relations on the one hand to the cosmogony in the *Timaeus*, and on the other hand to the polity sketched in the *Republic*, which itself has in Proclus a primarily ontological, rather than narrowly political value. Hence Proclus explains that the *Critias*, because it comes next in sequence after the *Timaeus*, "is composed by analogy with it, imparting in images the subsistence of the same things the primordial paradigms of which *Timaeus* has recounted through the demiurgy of the cosmos," (*PT* 5.21.76). But the *Timaeus*, in turn, begins by recapitulating the account of the eidetic structure of the state from the *Republic*, which was itself formulated in that dialogue primarily for the analogy it would offer to the structure of the soul. Since the cosmos is in the *Timaeus* given order by the demiurge through the constitution of the soul, the city in the *Republic* is in effect an image of the demiurge's work in the

Timaeus as much as it is an analogy of the soul's structure. But there is a city in the *Timaeus*, too, namely Atlantis, which features in this dialogue's account of the war between it and Athens. Proclus explains this by saying that the city-state outlined in the *Republic* and briefly recapitulated at the start of the *Timaeus* "pertains more to the heavens [*ton ouranon*], the war to generation, and hence the former is Zeus', while the latter pertains to Poseidon's allotment" (*IT* 1.206).

There is always a tension in Proclus implicit in the term *ouranos*, which refers to the heavens in a mundane, or even an astronomical sense, but which also cannot help but refer to Ouranos himself in a theological register. Poseidon's allotment is in a sense the very realm of Ouranos 'fallen' into the psycho-physical world, as we have seen. But since the realm allotted to Poseidon is, whether intrinsically or due to the position it assumes in the Olympian order, a realm constituted by motion, flux and change, it is symbolized in the *Timaeus*, the prior and therefore 'higher' dialogue, not as a polity, but as a war, a dynamic process, and only in the *Critias* is described in its stable form as a city-state. The Atlantean war, Proclus explains, should be understood "as existing in every nature. For the polity is analogous to Being and to essences, but war to the powers of those essences, and ... to their motions," (*IT* 1.78). Proclus goes on to apply this ontological interpretation of the Atlantean war to the account of theomachy, or strife among the Gods, in Homer (*Iliad* 21.385ff). In this interpretation, the specific Gods who are paired off against one another in the theomachy are explained with reference to the plane of Being they jointly constitute thereby, their conflict being ultimately a form of cooperative action. And so Poseidon and Apollon, who fight each other (435ff), do so "as the demiurges of the whole of generation, the one wholly, but the other partially," (*IT* 1.79). Poseidon and Apollon thus fashion, through their conflict, a conflictual plane of Being, namely our own plane of generation, of coming-to-be and passing away. It is appropriate, in this light, that Poseidon, in his speech to Apollon here (*Iliad* 21.441ff) reminds him of their joint labor under Laomedon to build up the city of Troy, Poseidon constructing the physical infrastructure of the city's wall and Apollon tending the city's herds, and hence building up the flesh of its citizens. Again we find that creation in the realm of generation is symbolically interchangeable with conflict, and hence Heraclitus is correct to say that "War is the father of all things" (frag. 53 Diels, quoted by Proclus at *IT* 1.76 and again at 1.174), as long as this is understood within its proper scope.

As cities identified with a war, and treated as symbolizing the conflictual realm of generation, Troy and Atlantis are virtual symbolic twins. According to a well-known interpretation, the name of Troy, Ilios, is taken to allude to the material plane (*hylê*): "By Ilion one must understand the generated and material place, which is named from mud [*ilun*]

225

and matter [*hylên*], and in which there is war and discord; and the Trojans are material forms, and all the lives around bodies," (Hermeas, In *Platonis Phaedrum* Couvreur (ed.), p. 77, trans. T. Taylor, mod.). As Proclus explains, "By Helen the myths signify all that beauty which as a result of demiurgy subsists around generation, concerning which there is a perpetual war of souls being waged, until the more intellective, having prevailed over the more irrational forms of life, return to the place whence they originally set out," (*In Remp.* 1.175).[7] Proclus characterizes in similar terms both the proxy conflict between Athena and Poseidon in the war between Athens and Atlantis, and the contest between these two Gods over Athens:

They [the Athenians] dedicated a festival to Athena, in consequence of her victory over Poseidon, and on account of the order of the principles active in generation [*tês genesiourgou taxeôs*] being mastered by the intellective [order] … For Poseidon presides over generation, but Athena is the overseer of intellective life … so that it is evident that the Atlantean war indicates the middle demiurgy, according to which the second father [Poseidon] being filled [*apoplêroumenos*] by Athena and the other invisible causes … subjects all things having a multiplied, divisible, and more material hypostasis to intellective natures. (*IT* 1.173)

The conflict between Athena and Poseidon, therefore, in whatever mythic context, expresses for Proclus a cooperation through conflict of these two Gods, a conflict which denotes not the subordination of one God to another, but rather the subjects of Poseidon's demiurgic activity coming conflictually, in accord with their nature, under Athena's oversight. When the end comes for the Atlanteans and for the Athenians of that era, they are said to succumb to deluge and to earthquakes respectively (*Tim.* 25cd), both "Poseidonian demiurgic actions" (*IT* 1.189.29-30), signifying that the entire theater of the conflict has been Poseidon's domain.

If the city of Troy is a symbol of the physical cosmos itself, then in laboring to construct its walls, Poseidon may be seen to be involved in fashioning the physical form of the living organism. In accord with his operation as demiurge of generation, it seems that Poseidon is especially associated with the transition into and out of the living form. Thus, Proclus notes, in his interpretation of the binding of Ares and Aphrodite by Hephaestus in the *Odyssey* (8.266ff), that Poseidon urges (344ff) Hephaestus to set them free, inasmuch as Poseidon "wills that the perpetuity of generation should be preserved, and the circle of change revolve into itself, that what comes to be should pass away, and what has passed away be sent back again to generation," (*In Remp.* 1.142.24-7).

This helps us to grasp a further important dimension of Poseidon's operations, namely his association with horses, which can be seen in a broader context of his involvement with the process of ensouling, and hence with the soul's 'vehicle' (*ochêma*). Plato attributes vehicles — chariots drawn by winged horses — to the Gods and to mortal souls alike in the *Phaedrus* (246a-248c), but the Gods are already given chariots in Homer, and the symbolism of the human soul and its powers as a complex of charioteer, chariot and team of horses, or of the soul in its embodied state as horse and rider according to diverse identifications, is widespread in Hellenic culture and in other cultures having perfected horsemanship.[8] To single out a particularly important example, the standard iconography of heroes depicts them accompanied either by horses or by snakes, which in shedding their skins exhibit a different aspect of the soul's relationship to its vehicle. It should also be noted that the Dioskouroi, who are in a way paradigmatic of the hero as such, in whom the hero's mortal and immortal aspects are differentiated into separate persons, are associated not only with horses, but also with ships, and hence with sea-going as well as terrestrial vehicles.[9]

With respect to the Gods themselves, Poseidon is said at *Iliad* 8.440 to unyoke (*luse*, with which compare Dionysos' epithet *lusaios*) the horses from Zeus' chariot when Zeus arrives at Olympos to attend a meeting of the Gods. Hermeas, in his commentary on Plato's *Phaedrus*, notes in relation to this that the Gods do not always ride or drive, and hence their chariots and horses are powers they exercise at some times and not at others (122.27-123.3). Nor need the vehicle or mount of a God be a horse or chariot, of course. The theology of divine *vahanas*, vehicles or mounts, is highly developed in Hinduism, in which generally speaking every deity has some animal as their *vahana*, a psychical power they project into the world. Poseidon's action with respect to Zeus' vehicle in the *Iliad* passage suggests that Poseidon, as master of horses, has a role in relation to this broader divine function. In Platonic taxonomy divine souls are *daimons*, of whom Proclus remarks, in connection with *Parm.* 126c, that

the agencies that order the life of souls in the world of generation ... we ordinarily call divine daemons. The occupation of horsemanship is a fitting symbol of their activity ... [they] hold nature together by serving as front-runners or bodyguards or followers of the Gods. For they are in a way charioteers, and in them there are 'horses', as there are among the Gods ... There are, then, 'horses' among the Gods as well, and the art of horsemanship in the primary sense. But on that level the horses are to an extreme degree united with the charioteer, while on the daemonic level they are distinct, and there is a greater degree of otherness, so that the directing

229

element appears and is one thing, and the 'horses' another ... The daemons are at home in the rank of the Gods because of the intermediate station they occupy; for Poseidon occupies an intermediate rank among the Fathers, even as daemons do among the classes superior to us. (*In Parm.* 674-5, trans. Morrow and Dillon)

The specific reference to Poseidon here is occasioned by the text's reference to Melite, which takes its name from a consort of Poseidon's. Poseidon in this passage is at once analogous to the *daimons* themselves, mediators between the Gods and mortals, in his position of middle demiurge, while also, as master of divine 'horses', operating across the ranks of Gods, *daimons* and mortals insofar as each of these have spiritual 'vehicles' of one kind or another, and with the different kinds of relations among their parts Proclus describes.

Through his sovereignty over change, over the soul realm, and over the relation to the vehicle, Poseidon has a role for Platonists in eschatology going beyond what is apparent from what we know of Hellenic theology. The reason for this discrepancy is largely to be attributed to the centrality of reincarnation for the Platonists. Hence, when Damascius explains, in his commentary on the *Phaedo*, that "The destinations of souls are threefold: prior to genesis in the realm of Zeus, in genesis in the realm of Poseidon, after genesis in the realm of Pluto," (I §470) it is not only a question of

Poseidon ruling over this life here and now, but also over the process of coming to birth again. And so, when Plato in the *Republic*'s Myth of Er speaks of the souls coming from above and from below to the place where they will choose new lives for themselves (614de), Proclus explains that they are coming either from the place of Zeus or that of Hades to the place of Poseidon (*In Remp.* 2.156). When the souls come to birth in Er's account, it is with "a sound of thunder and a quaking of the earth" that they are "wafted thence, one this way, one that, upward to their birth like shooting stars" (*Rep.* 621b), and Proclus explains the thunder and earthquake as signifying "the demiurgic operations that Zeus and Poseidon perform together, from above and from below, upon generation" (In *Remp.* 2.95). "For as the descent is made from the heavens to the earth, from the place of Zeus to that of Poseidon, the thunderclap, coming from above, has been adopted as symbol of Zeus' working, the earthquake as symbolizing Poseidon's demiurgy, as if these two demiurgies join together to aid our descent into genesis," (ibid., 2.351f). Poseidon's seismic power seems even more intimately associated with the process of coming into the world in Proclus' remark in his *Platonic Theology* (6.10.46f) that "Poseidon is allotted hollow and cavernous places, in which generation, motion, and tremors come about. Hence, they call this God 'earth-shaker'."

231

It is perhaps worth noting in conclusion that in the 1580s, John Dee and others in his circle routinely referred to the new continent across the Atlantic as 'Atlantis', during the same era in which Giordano Bruno glorified Queen Elizabeth in his esoteric writings as 'Amphitrite'. The utopian speculations that attached themselves to the new land in the European imagination, therefore, may perhaps in some sense be regarded as further expressions of an alternative Poseidonian sovereignty, which would hold the promise of overturning the static European social and metaphysical order from its periphery, an Atlantis bringing not conquest this time, but revolution. The late Byzantine scholar and revolutionary Gemistos Plethon (1355-1452/4), who advocated a return to the worship of the Olympian Gods, perhaps foreshadowed this by the prominence he accords to Poseidon in his works, where Poseidon, as the second highest god after Zeus, organizes the intelligible world of the forms and is the form of Form, Form Itself.[10] Hladky, in his major study of Plethon's thought, finds Poseidon's exalted status in it "most puzzling" (113), but we can see that beginning from the interpretation of the ancient Platonists, who treated the division of the Kronian sovereignty as a total division of Being, it is a simple, if idiosyncratic step to Plethon's formulation. The position accorded to Poseidon in Plethon's philosophical theology in this way tells us something important about Plethon's own project, for it reveals it to be not a conservative return to a Hellenic past, but rather a glimpse, from within the renewed horizon of Hellenic theophany, of a new intellectual age, in which motion, change, diversity, and psychology were to exert the dominant influence, as thought sets itself forth upon the "boundless sea of dissimilitude" (Plato, *Statesman* 273d).

Notes:

1) *PT* = Proclus, *Platonic Theology*: H. D. Saffrey & L. G. Westerink, (edd. & trans.), *Proclus: Théologie platonicienne*, 6 vols. (Paris: Les Belles Lettres, 1968-1997).

2) *ET* = Proclus, *Elements of Theology*: E. R. Dodds (ed. & trans.), *The Elements of Theology*, 2nd ed. (Oxford: Clarendon Press, 1963).

3) *IT* = Proclus, *In Platonis Timaeum commentaria*: E. Diehl, (ed.), *Procli Diadochi In Platonis Timaeum commentaria* (Leipzig: Teubner, 1903-1906). Translations based on T. Taylor, *Proclus' Commentary on the Timaeus of Plato* (Frome, Somerset: Prometheus Trust, 1998) [1816], freely modified.

4) L. G. Westerink (ed. & trans.), *Damascius: Commentary on Plato's Phaedo*, 2nd ed. (Westbury, Wiltshire: Prometheus Trust, 2009).

5) See my "Queen of Kinêsis: Understanding Hera," pp. 126-148 in Lykeia (ed.), *Queen of Olympos: A Devotional Anthology for Hera and Iuno* (Asheville, NC: Bibliotheca Alexandrina, 2013).

6) Nor is this perspective confined to the space of Hellenic theology, either, as can be seen from the importance of water-based cosmogony, with the symbolic equation of water with indeterminate motion and flux, in Egyptian theology and philosophy, on which see my remarks in "Opening the Way of Writing: Semiotic Metaphysics in the *Book of Thoth*," esp. pp. 217-221. (In A. D. DeConick, G. Shaw, and J. D. Turner (edd.), *Practicing Gnosis: Ritual, Magic, Theurgy and Liturgy in Nag Hammadi, Manichaean and Other Ancient Literature. Essays in Honor of Birger A. Pearson* (Leiden: Brill, 2013).)

7) *In Remp.* = Proclus, *In Platonis rem publicam commentarii*, W. Kroll (ed.), trans. A. J. Festugière, *Proclus: Commentaire sur la république*, 3 vols. (Paris: Vrin, 1970).

8) On the symbolism of the horse in Hellenic thought generally, with particular attention to Poseidon's and Athena's distinct relations to horsemanship, see "The Live Bit", pp. 187-214 in M. Detienne and J.-P. Vernant, *Cunning Intelligence in Greek Culture and Society*, trans. J. Lloyd (Chicago, IL: University of Chicago Press, 1991).

9) On the Dioskouroi, see my essay "The Ashwins and the Dioskouroi: A Theological Comparison," in *Megaloi Theoi: A Devotional Anthology for the Dioskouroi and Helen of Troy*, ed. John Drury (Bibliotheca Alexandrina, forthcoming).

10) Vojtech Hladky, *The Philosophy of Gemistos Plethon: Platonism in Late Byzantium, between Hellenism and Orthodoxy* (Farnham, Surrey: Ashgate, 2014), pp. 98-99.

To Poseidon Gaiêokhos

by Terence Ward

It is the whole world, Gaiêokhos,
that depends on your protection, Gaiêokhos.
The trust of the whole planet, Gaiêokhos,
is in the holder of the earth.

The plants that are budding, Gaiêokhos,
and the deer who are rutting, Gaiêokhos,
all that's green, all that's growing, Gaiêokhos
trusts the holder of the earth.

Gaea loves her children, Gaiêokhos,
from the youthful to decrepit, Gaiêokhos,
and to you she trusts their future, Gaiêokhos,
as the holder of the earth.

We do not have the foresight, Gaiêokhos,
for progress without damage, Gaiêokhos, so
from ourselves we ask protection, Gaiêokhos,
so we don't destroy the earth.

It is the whole world, Gaiêokhos,
that depends on your protection, Gaiêokhos.
The trust of the whole planet, Gaiêokhos,
is in the holder of the earth.

Poseidon's Alchemy

by Christina Murphy

The over-ripe warmth of a dim
indigo in a loom of starlight
shining across pebbles in the river

A rider appears in the glorious gold
of a wild horse's sheen drawn from
the fields and sea into numinous mystery

The river and the rider merge and emerge
into the beauty of water moving with unseen
currents of mystical power reshaping the moment

The waters crest and bring the sea-goddess
to inhabit the night with silver and gold
filaments of graceful light and crystal forms

In graveyards nearby, the bones of dreamers
lie in darkness, the metamorphosis of spirit
that glides through luminous night skies

Once there was the solace of Poseidon's alchemy
to change the heart, change the soul, make the seas
into a loom of chance as storms rattled the sky-
        winds

Once the earth trembled and split with the energy of
a proud god wrapped in visions of triumph and
   destiny
and the sky reflected the magnitude of the
   disruptions

In the immensity of time, the currents of change
   shaped
by Poseidon reappear on indigo and silver nights as
   the rider
of a golden horse traversing the skies that once were
   seas

And even starlight yields to Poseidon's majestic
   power,
creating bits of light, sharp with trident points, to
   fill
the waves of infinite night with the glory of
   remembrance

"Poseidon" by Callum Hurley

Appendix A: Greek Spirits of the Sea

[Note: the Greeks were and are a sea-faring culture. As such, their mythology is rich with Gods and Goddesses and spirits of the sea, rivers, clouds, and sky. Below is a list of a very few of these Deities, who are specifically named in this anthology.]

Amphitrite: Queen of the sea, especially the Aegean. Daughter of either Nereus or Okeanus. Wife of Poseidon and mother of Triton, among other Deities.

Aphrodite: Goddess of love and lust and beauty. In some genealogies, she was born when the severed genitals of Kronos mixed with the sea; thus her epithets, "Sea-Born" and "Foam-Born."

Doris: An Okeanid. By Nereus, she is the mother of the Nereides. Possibly Goddess of the rich fishing-grounds which can be found at the mouths of rivers.

Electra: An Okeanid, possibly a Nephele (cloud nymph). Mother of Iris and the Harpies by Thaumas.

Eurynome: The Titan Goddess of water-meadows and pasturelands. Daughter of Okeanos and Tethys, and mother of the Charites by Zeus.

Graeae (Graiai): Ancient sea daemones, they shared a single tooth and a single eye among themselves. Two or three in number, they were consulted by Perseus in his hunt for Medusa.

Harpies (Harpyiai): The spirits of sudden, sharp wind; called the Hounds of Zeus. Usually depicted as either winged women, or women with the bodies of birds. Daughters of Thaumas and Electra, sisters of Iris.

Iris: Goddess of the rainbow and messenger of the Gods, especially Hera. She fetches the waters of Styx when the Gods need to make a binding oath. Daughter of Thaumas and Electra, sister of the Harpies.

Kybele (Cybele): The Phrygian mother of the Gods; often equated with Rhea, the Titan mother of the Gods, sister-wife of Kronos, and mother of Poseidon.

Medusa (Medousa): A Gorgon, either loved or raped by Poseidon. Perseus slew her and threw her head into the sea, where it continues to roll across the bottom, creating coral.

Naiades (Naiads): Freshwater nymphs who inhabit rivers, lakes, streams, fountains, marshes, and springs; sometimes considered a subgroup within the Okeanides. They are further subdivided into categories based on the natural feature which they inhabit: Pegaiai (springs), Krenaiai (fountains), Potameides (rivers), Limnades (lakes), Heleionomai (marshes and wetlands). They are often honored as Goddesses of pregnancy, fertility, healing, and prophecy. Daughters of Okeanos and/or the male Potameides (river Gods).

Neptune (Neptunus): Roman God of the sea; often equated with Poseidon. Husband of Salacia.

Nereides: The fifty daughters of Nereus and Doris. They watch over fishermen and sailors, and care for the riches of the sea.

Nereus: The old man of the sea. A master shapeshifter. Husband of Doris and father of the fifty Nereides.

Okeanides (Oceanides): The three thousand daughters of Okeanos and Tethys who preside over the world's fresh water. The Naiades are among their number, as are the Nephelai (cloud nymphs), Aurai (wind spirits), Leimonides (pasture nymphs), and Anthousai (flower spirits). The more famous Okeanides include Doris (mother of the Nereides), Electra (mother of Iris), Eurynome (mother of the Charites), Metis (mother of Athena), and Styx (underworld river).

Okeanos (Oceanus): Primeval God of the river which encircles the world; source of all freshwater. Husband of Tethys and father of the three thousand Okeanides.

Poseidon: The great Olympian God of the sea, rivers, earthquakes, floods, drought, and horses. Husband of Amphitrite, and father of Triton, among many other Deities and heroes.

Proteus: Ancient sea God, known for his gift of prophecy. Herdsman of seals.

Styx: Goddess of the underworld river of the same name. One of the Okeanides, a daughter of Okeanos and Tethys. The Gods swear by her holy water.

Tethys: The Titan Goddess of fresh, subterranean waters. Mother of the Okeanides by Okeanos.

Thaumas: An ancient sea God who personifies the wonders of the ocean. Husband of Electra, and father of Iris and the Harpies.

Triton: The fish-tailed son and herald of Poseidon and Amphitrite. He is often depicted with a conch shell trumpet. The Tritones as a group, who make up part of the entourage of Poseidon, were named in his honor.

Appendix B: Epithets and Cults Sites of Poseidon

compiled by Chelsea Luellon Bolton

Epithets
Aigaiôn (of the Aegean Sea)
Aspheleios (Steadfast)
Asphalios (Secures Safe Voyage)
Basileus (King)
Dômatitês (of the House)
Ennosigaios (Earth-Shaker)
Epoptês (Overseer, Watcher)
Gaieokhos (Earth-Holder)
Genethlios (of the Kin; Kindred)
Hippios (of Horses)
Hippokourios (Horse Tender)
Laoitês (of the People)
Pater (Father)
Patros (Father, Ancestral)
Pelagaios (of the Sea)
Petraios (of the Rock)
Phutalmios (Nourishing)
Phytalmios (Plant Nurturer)
Prosklystios (Who Dashes Against)
Soter (Savior)
Taureos (Bull-like)

Cult Centers
Aigaios (Of Aigai in Euboia)
Genesios (Of Genesion in Argolis)

Helikônios (Of Mt Helicon in Boiotia)
Isthmios (Of the Isthmus of Korinthos)
Onkhêsios (Of Onkhesto in Boiotia)
Samios (Of Samos in Elis & the Island)
Tainarios (Of Tainaron in Lakonia)

Temple and Festivals
Poseidion or Poseidônion (Temple of Poseidon)
Poseidônia (Festival of Poseidon)
Isthmia (Isthmian Festival)
Pharia (8 Audçnaios)
Theoxenia Aethiopia (8 Gorpiaios)

Sources
Poseidon at Theoi.com
Poseidon at Neos Alexandria

Appendix C: Our Contributors

Mary Ann Back lives in Mason, Ohio, with her husband, Pete and her beloved dog, Max. She is a Pushcart Prize nominee and was awarded the 2009 Bilbo Award for creative writing by Thomas More College. The characters she creates are often disreputable and not to be trusted. She kicks them to the curb every chance she gets when some unwitting publisher agrees to take them off her hands. Her writing has appeared in many publications, including: *Short Story America, Every Day Fiction, Bete Noire, Apollo's Lyre, Liquid Imagination, 50 to 1, Legends*, and *A Twist of Noir*. Her first short story anthology, *Dead Reckoning*, is available through *Grey Wolfe Publishing*.

Jeffrey Beck is the recent winner of the Hart Crane Memorial Poetry Award, honorable mention winner of the Frank O'Hara Poetry Prize, and finalist in the *Naugatuck River Review* poetry award. His poetry has been published or will be published in *Miramar, Worcester Review, Grey Sparrow Journal, I-70 Review, Cold Mountain Review, Blue Lyra Review, Sow's Ear Poetry Review*, and other journals. The author of four books of prose, he is at work on his first book of poetry, *Travel Kit for Odyssey*.

With an interest in the occult and all things mythical spanning over 25 years, **Frances Billinghurst** is also a prolific writer with articles and essays appearing in over 20 separate publications, including Llewellyn's *Witch's Calendar*, *The Cauldron*, *Unto Herself: A Devotional Anthology to Independent Goddesses*, *A Mantle of Stars: A Devotional to the Queen of Heaven*, and *The Faeries Queens*. She is the author of *Dancing the Sacred Wheel: A Journey through the Southern Sabbats* and *In her Sacred Name: Writings on the Divine Feminine*, and is currently editing a devotional anthology of the various guises of the Divine Masculine found within modern Paganism. Details of what Frances gets up to in her spare time can be found on the Temple of the Dark Moon's web site (www.templedarkmoon.com) or The Goddess House blog (http://thegoddesshouse.blogspot.com.au).

Amanda Sioux Blake opted not to provide a biography.

Chelsea Luellon Bolton has a BA and MA in Religious Studies from the University of South Florida. She has been dedicated to the ancient Egyptian Goddess Aset for over a decade. Her poetry has been previously published in various anthologies. You can read more of her work at her blog at fiercelybrightone.com.

Melia Brokaw is a Librarian, Housewife, Mother, Wife, Devotee to Zeus and Isis, Writer, Crafter and

Woman. She is an octopus with many tentacles of interest making her way through the sea of life. Editor of *From Cave to Sky*, another book in the *Biblotheca Alexandrina* line up, under the name Melia Suez.

Personal Blog: 4ofwands.wordpress.com.

Author Blog: OakenScrolls.wordpress.com.

Rebecca Buchanan is the editor-in-chief of *Bibliotheca Alexandrina*. She is also editor of the Pagan literary ezine, Eternal Haunted Summer. She has been published in a variety of venues, including *Bards and Sages Quarterly, Cliterature, Hex Magazine, Luna Station Quarterly, New Realm*, and *T Gene Davis' Speculative Fiction Blog*, among others.

Edward Butler received his doctorate from the New School for Social Research in 2004 for his dissertation "The Metaphysics of Polytheism in Proclus". Since then, he has published numerous articles in academic journals and edited volumes, as well as contributing essays to several devotional volumes. He writes a regular column, Noēseis, for Polytheist.com, and is a co-editor of *Walking the Worlds: A Biannual Journal of Polytheism and Spiritwork*. He also has a strong interest in Egyptian theology, and has written entries on over one hundred and fifty Egyptian deities for his "Theological Encyclopedia of the Goddesses and

Gods of the Ancient Egyptians", which he hosts on his site, Henadology: Philosophy and Theology (henadology.wordpress.com), where more information about his work can be found.

Cailin is and will always be in awe of the vast and glorious sea.

Jolene Dawe is a polytheist devoted to Poseidon and Odin. She is the author of *Treasure from the Deep*, a collection of Poseidon's myths retold, and *The Fairy Queen of Spencer's Butte and Other Tales*, a collection of tales inspired by and set in and around the Willamette Valley. You can find her blogging at Strip Me Back to the Bone on Wordpress, where she talks about life, writing, Poseidon, cats, knitting, and Poseidon.

Natasha Handy is Hellenic Polytheist of five years and has been residing in Scotland, North Ayrshire, but has also lived in London for ten. Having previously lived most of her childhood and teen life in Spain, she is a fluent Spanish speaker and also knows some french having lived in the lush tropical island of Seychelles for two years. She devotes her time to cub scouting and is a warranted Cubscout Leader by the name of Baloo the Bear as well as helping out at beavers, to which she believes helps her connect with both the God Apollo and Goddess Artemis, respectively. She is the founder of four

Facebook groups devoted to Lords Ares (Shrine of Ares), Hephaestus (Shrine of Hephaestus) and Poseidon (Shrine of Poseidon), but her main group is "Celebrating Hellenic Altars", of which she is very proud. Her first devotional writing has also appeared in the book *Harnessing Fire: A Devotional Anthology in Honor of Hephaestus*. She can be contacted through her facebook groups or her email at natasha_handy@hotmail.com

Michael Hardy is a member of ar n'Draiocht Fein (ADF) who lives near Washington D.C., and a member of CedarLight Grove (ADF) in Baltimore, Md. He is working toward ordination as an ADF priest. Hermes was the Hellenic god who first drew his attention, but he has since heard the call of many others.

Ann Hatzakis writes: There's not much to tell. I'm a Hellenic Polytheist and a mommy. I write things so that my daughter and other kids can hopefully understand more than I could when I started on this path.

Sandy Hiortdahl lives with Kismo Blue, an Australian Cattle Dog, in East Tennessee. She's a recipient of the Sophie Kerr Prize, The Maryland State Governor's Award for Literary Excellence, and The Ghost Mountain Award. She has an M.F.A. from George Mason and a Ph.D. from The Catholic

University of America. Her work has appeared this year in *THEMA*, *The Summerset Review* and *Barely South Review*, among others. She regularly attends the John Gardner Conference and The Key West Literary Seminar. More may be found on her website: www.sandyhiortdahl.com She's on Twitter: @hiortdahl

Juleigh Howard-Hobson's work has appeared in *Idunna*, *Hex Magazine*, *NewWitch*, *Megalithic Poetry*, *The Old Heathen's Almanac*, *Mjolnir*, *The Runepebble*, *Into the Willows*, *Enchanted Conversation*, *The Liar's League*, *The ORB*, *The AFA Voice*, *Odin's Gift*, *Primordial Traditions*, *Northern Traditions*, *Umbrella* (the faith issue), *Soundzine* (the luck issue), *The Journal of Contemporary Heathen Thought* Volume 1 (*Heithen Publications*), *Mandragora* (*Scarlet Imprint*), *The Asatru Folk Assembly's Runestone Journal* Volume 1 (which she edited as well), and is forthcoming in *Daughter of the Sun: A Devotional Anthology in Honor of Sekhmet* (*Bibliotheca Alexandrina*).

Ann Howells's poetry appears in *Borderlands, Concho River Review*, *Crannog* (Ire*)*, *Plainsongs, RiverSedge, San Pedro River Review* and *Spillway* among others. She serves on the board of Dallas Poets Community, 501-c-3 non-profit, and has edited *Illya's Honey*, since 1999, recently going digital (www.IllyasHoney.com). Her chapbooks are, *Black Crow in Flight*, (Main Street Rag, 2007) and *the Rosebud Diaries* (Willet Press, 2012). She has been read on NPR, interviewed on *Writers Around Annapolis* television, and been four times nominated for a Pushcart, twice in 2014.

Hello to all, my name is **Callum Hurley** and I'm a Biology graduate from the University of Sheffield in Yorkshire, England. Whist I might be a scientist by profession, I have had an abiding love of both Poetry and Mythology from a young age, but have only in recent years begun to think more philosophically about my twin passions and pursue new theological lines of reasoning. This has led me to recognise myself as an eclectic polytheist, who looks for truth and meaning in many myths and paths, though I must confess that I am particularly fond of Greek thought having spent many months there throughout my childhood years. I am a big admirer of the work done at New Alexandria and hope to continue to enjoy and support them in the future. If you'd like to get in touch I'm always happy to hear from you at callumhurley@hotmail.com.

Darius M. Klein is a translator, writer, and independent scholar currently residing in Indianapolis, Indiana. His works of creative mythology have appeared in *Eternal Haunted Summer*, *Niteblade*, and *Beyond the Pillars: An Anthology of Pagan Fantasy*. He has worked with Ouroboros Press and other contemporary publishers of Hermetic/Occult books to produce quality translations of Alchemical texts, and his translations have contributed to research in the field of the history of science. Details concerning his work can be found at https://independent.academia.edu/DariusKlein.

Steve Klepetar's work has received several nominations for the Pushcart Prize and Best of the Net, including three in 2014. Recent collections include *Speaking to the Field Mice* (*Sweatshoppe Publications*), *My Son Writes a Report on the Warsaw Ghetto* (*Flutter Press*) and *Return of the Bride of Frankenstein* (*Kind of a Hurricane Press*).

Nina Kossman is a poet, artist, writer, and playwright. The recipient of a National Endowment for the Arts fellowship, a UNESCO/PEN Short Story Award, grants from the Foundation for Hellenic Culture and Alexander S. Onassis Public Benefit Foundation, she has translated two books of Marina Tsvetaeva's poetry. Two books of her Russian poems were published in Moscow. Her other publications include *Behind the Border* (*HarperCollins*, 1994) and *Gods and Mortals: Modern Poems on Classical Myths*. She lives in New York.

Jennifer Lawrence likes doing things the hard way, which explains most of how her life has turned out. Her interests include history, gardening, herbalism, mythology and fairy tales, hiking, camping, and the martial arts. Her work has appeared in numerous publications, including many devotional anthologies. A multi-trad pagan, she has followed the gods of Greece, Ireland, and the Northlands for decades now; she is a member of Hellenion, The Troth, Ár nDraíocht Féin, and Ord Brigideach. She lives with five cats, an overgrown garden full of nature spirits, an ossuary full of skulls, and a houseful of gargoyles somewhere outside of Chicago.

Lykeia is a priestess of Apollon, serving him through inspired poetry, and research, as well as various mediums of art. All that she creates she does as a manner of praise to him. Her work presented in honor of Bast honors the beauty and dignity of the goddess who she has held in awe since childhood.

Hillary Lyon lives in southern Arizona, where she is the founder of and editor for **Subsynchronous Press**, publisher of two poetry journals (*The Laughing Dog*, and *Veil: Journal of Darker Musings*). She holds an MA in English Lit from Southern Methodist University. Her stories and poems have appeared in hundreds of publications, both online and in print. She appeared, briefly, as the uncredited "all-American Mom with baby" in Timothy Gassen's Arizona indie-film, *Vote for Zombie*.

Australian artist, **Wayne McMillan** is known locally for his mythological subject matter, often presented to the public as street art.

Mari is a Hellenic polytheist residing in New Orleans, Louisiana. Given the city's precarious relationship with water, she considers devotion to Poseidon a practical matter as well as a personal one. She has been writing poetry for nearly two decades and, in 2014, she released a collection of devotional poems and prayers for the gods of Hellenic polytheism. *Glories* is available through Lulu.com as both an ebook and a paperback.

Emily May is a writer and illustrator from South London with a fascination for mythology, mysticism and the human spirit. Having dabbled in journalism and illustration within the fashion industry for several years, and subsequently rejected it, she is now creating dark and frightening children's tales and poetry.

Bella Michel comes from a small town in Colorado where she currently resides. Attending the University of Denver as a Information Technology major, she wishes to one day return to school to learn about art. She knows Spanish, Russian and English and is a first generation American. While her dream of dreams is to become a professional poet, she knows that regardless of what happens she will continue to pursue her art for a long time.

Christina Murphy's poetry is an exploration of consciousness as subjective experience, and her poems appear in a wide range of journals and anthologies, including, in *PANK, La Fovea, Dali's Lovechild*, and *Hermeneutic Chaos Literary Journal*, and in the anthologies *Let the Sea Find its Edges* and *Remaking Moby-Dick.* Her work has twice been nominated for the Pushcart Prize and for the *Best of the Net Anthology*.

With his first collection of poetry, *Manhattan Plaza*, **James B. Nicola** joins poets Elizabeth Bishop, Frank O'Hara and Stanley Kunitz and humorist Robert Benchley as a New York author hailing from Worcester. His second poetry collection, *Stage to Page: Poems from the Theater*, is scheduled for publication in 2016. He was represented in *Harnessing Fire* by *Bibliotheca Alexandrina*. A Yale grad and stage director by profession, his non-fiction book *Playing the Audience* won a Choice award. Also a composer, lyricist, and playwright, James's children's musical *Chimes: A Christmas Vaudeville* premiered in Fairbanks, Alaska, where Santa Claus was rumored to be in attendance on opening night.

Rachel V. Olivier is a writer and copy editor and proofreader. Her poetry and fiction may be found in various places, including *Everyday Weirdness, Daily Love, Aoife's Kiss, Electric Velocipede and Bewildering Stories*. You may also check out some of her work (or hire her for copy editing/ proofreading jobs) at her site, Putt Putt Productions.

Rachel Petersen writes: I have been a Solitary Eclectic Pagan since Samhain 2011; I work mainly with the ancient Greek pantheon, but I am also building a form of neo-totemism involving skin spirits. Though it was Artemis who introduced me to Paganism, Iris quickly took over as my "patron deity." I try not to be pushy about it, but I enjoy every chance I get to tell others about such a beautiful Goddess as Iris. I took the surname Iriswings as a sign of devotion to Her, and I am grateful for the lessons and inspiration that She brings me every day.

Ruby Sara is the editor of two collections of esoteric poetry published by *Scarlet Imprint* (*Datura*, 2010 and *Mandragora*, 2012). Her work has been included most recently in two theatre productions at The VORTEX Repertory Company (EARTH, 2013, and SPIRIT, 2014), and in 2013 her poem "the woman who caught a storm in her hair" was nominated for a Rhysling Award from the Science Fiction Poetry Association. She lives in

Austin, TX with her intrepid spouse and their demon-monkey-cat, Pinky.

Shoshana Sarah is an American born poet, English teacher, collage artist, amateur dancer, and the creator of Poets of Babel, a multilingual poetry club. A lover of languages, she speaks Hebrew, French, and Russian, and has studied others just for kicks. She established Poets of Babel as a sneaky way to combine her two greatest loves: languages and poetry. Her publications appear in the fall 2011 issues of *The Ilanot Review, Yes, Poetry,* in the 2012 winter edition of *Eternal Haunted Summer,* in the August 2013 issue of فضاء الـ מרחב *space* and *Mixed Race 3.0: Risk and Reward in the Digital Age*.

Suzanne Thackston is a Hellenic polytheist, a ceremonial magician, a Demetrian priestess, a homeschooling mom emerita, a tender of old horses and other assorted orphan creatures, a devoted but inept gardener, a wishful cook, a reader, a seeker, a dreamer, a fitful writer, and an endlessly curious student of the world, the universe, the gods, and everything.

John J. Trause, the Director of Oradell Public Library, is the author of *Eye Candy for Andy (13 Most Beautiful... Poems for Andy Warhol's Screen Tests*, Finishing Line Press, 2013); *Inside Out,*

Upside Down, and Round and Round (Nirala Publications, 2012); the chapbook *Seriously Serial* (Poets Wear Prada, 2007; rev. ed. 2014); and *Latter-Day Litany* (Éditions élastiques, 1996), the latter staged Off-Off Broadway. His translations, poetry, and visual work appear internationally in many journals and anthologies, including the artists' periodical *Crossings*, the Dada journal *Maintenant*, the journal *Offerta Speciale*, the Uphook Press anthologies *Hell Strung and Crooked* and *-gape-seed-*, and the Great Weather for Media anthologies *It's Animal but Merciful* (2012) and *I Let Go of the Stars in My Hand* (2014) as well as in *Potnia: A Devotional Anthology in Honor of Demeter* (Bibliotheca Alexandrina, 2014). Marymark Press has published his visual poetry and art as broadsides and sheets. He has shared the stage with Steven Van Zandt, Anne Waldman, Karen Finley, and Jerome Rothenberg, the page with Lita Hornick, William Carlos Williams, Woody Allen, Ted Kooser, and Pope John Paul II, and the cage with the Cumaean Sibyl, Ezra Pound, Hannibal Lector, Andrei Chikatilo, and George "The Animal" Steele. He is a founder of the William Carlos Williams Poetry Cooperative in Rutherford, N. J., and the former host and curator of its monthly reading series. He has been nominated for the Pushcart Prize (2009 – 2011, 2013).]

Bill Vernon served in the United States Marine Corps, studied English literature, then taught it. Writing is his therapy, along with exercising outdoors and doing international folkdances. His poems, stories and nonfiction have appeared in a variety of magazines and anthologies. Speculative stories have appeared in *Rogue Worlds; From Beyond; Fantasy Today; Fables; Planet Magazine*; and other magazines. *Five Star Mysteries* published his novel *Old Town* in 2005.

Terence P. Ward realized he was Pagan after he bought his own copy of *Drawing Down the Moon* in 1988. His religious practices since have included being bound to a Wiccan coven, walking sacred trails as a backpacking Pagan or Gaiaped, raising energy with a number of loosely-organized collections of people, and being tapped by the Olympian gods. He is a polytheist with pantheistic and monistic sympathies, an animist approach to the world, and a respect for his ancestors. His personal practice includes daily offerings to Poseidon and weekly meeting for worship with his fellow Quakers.

Matthew Wilson, 31, has had over 150 appearances in such places as *Horror Zine, Star*Line, Spellbound, Illumen, Apokrupha Press, Hazardous Press, Gaslight Press, Sorcerers Signal* and many more. He is currently editing his first novel and can be contacted on twitter @matthew94544267.

About Bibliotheca Alexandrina

Ptolemy Soter, the first Makedonian ruler of Egypt, established the library at Alexandria to collect all of the world's learning in a single place. His scholars compiled definitive editions of the Classics, translated important foreign texts into Greek, and made monumental strides in science, mathematics, philosophy and literature. By some accounts over a million scrolls were housed in the famed library, and though it has long since perished due to the ravages of war, fire, and human ignorance, the image of this great institution has remained as a powerful inspiration down through the centuries.

To help promote the revival of traditional polytheistic religions we have launched a series of books dedicated to the ancient gods of Greece and Egypt. The library is a collaborative effort drawing on the combined resources of the different elements within the modern Hellenic and Kemetic communities, in the hope that we can come together to praise our gods and share our diverse understandings, experiences and approaches to the divine.

A list of our current and forthcoming titles can be found on the following page. For more information on the Bibliotheca, our submission requirements for upcoming devotionals, or to learn about our organization, please visit us at neosalexandria.org.

Sincerely,

The Editorial Board
of the Library of Neos Alexandria

Current Titles

Written in Wine: A Devotional Anthology for Dionysos

Dancing God: Poetry of Myths and Magicks

Goat Foot God

Longing for Wisdom: The Message of the Maxims

The Phillupic Hymns

Unbound: A Devotional Anthology for Artemis

Waters of Life: A Devotional Anthology for Isis and Serapis

Bearing Torches: A Devotional Anthology for Hekate

Queen of the Great Below: An Anthology in Honor of Ereshkigal

From Cave to Sky: A Devotional Anthology in Honor of Zeus

Out of Arcadia: A Devotional Anthology for Pan

Anointed: A Devotional Anthology for the Deities of the Near and Middle East

The Scribing Ibis: An Anthology of Pagan Fiction in Honor of Thoth

Queen of the Sacred Way: A Devotional Anthology in Honor of Persephone

Unto Herself: A Devotional Anthology for Independent Goddesses

The Shining Cities: An Anthology of Pagan Science Fiction

Guardian of the Road: A Devotional Anthology in Honor of Hermes

Harnessing Fire: A Devotional Anthology in Honor of Hephaestus

Beyond the Pillars: An Anthology of Pagan Fantasy

Queen of Olympos: A Devotional Anthology for Hera and Iuno

A Mantle of Stars: A Devotional Anthology in Honor of the Queen of Heaven

Crossing the River: An Anthology in Honor of Sacred Journeys

Ferryman of Souls: A Devotional for Charon

By Blood, Bone, and Blade: A Tribute to the Morrigan

Potnia: An Anthology in Honor of Demeter

The Queen of the Sky Who Rules Over All the Gods: A Devotional Anthology in Honor of Bast

From the Roaring Deep: A Devotional for Poseidon and the Spirits of the Sea

Forthcoming Titles

Daughter of the Sun: A Devotional Anthology in Honor of Sekhmet

Seasons of Grace: A Devotional in Honor of the Mousai, the Charites, and the Horae

Garland of the Goddess: Tales and Poems of the Feminine Divine

Les Cabinet des Polythéistes: An Anthology of Pagan Fairy Tales, Fables, and Nursery Rhymes

Shield of Wisdom: A Devotional Anthology in Honor of Athena

Megaloi Theoi: A Devotional Anthology for the Dioskouroi and Their Families

Sirius Rising: A Devotional Anthology for Cynocephalic Deities

46007102R00150

Made in the USA
San Bernardino, CA
23 February 2017